T0277183

Craveworthy Baking

Quarto.com

© 2024 Quarto Publishing Group USA Inc.
Text © 2024 Danielle Cochran

First Published in 2024 by Fair Winds Press, an imprint of The Quarto Group,
100 Cummings Center, Suite 265-D, Beverly, MA 01915, USA.
T (978) 282-9590 F (978) 283-2742

Fair Winds Press titles are also available at discount for retail, wholesale, promotional, and bulk purchase. For details, contact the Special Sales Manager by email at specialsales@quarto.com or by mail at The Quarto Group, Attn: Special Sales Manager, 100 Cummings Center, Suite 265-D, Beverly, MA 01915, USA.

28 27 26 25 24   1 2 3 4 5

ISBN: 978-0-7603-8847-1

Digital edition published in 2024
eISBN: 978-0-7603-8848-8

Library of Congress Cataloging-in-Publication Data is available.

Design: Laura Klynstra
Photography: Arrae Photography

Printed in China

The information in this book is for educational purposes only. It is not intended to replace the advice of a physician or medical practitioner. Please see your health-care provider before beginning any new health program.

Craveworthy Baking

Delicious Dairy-Free and Gluten-Free Cakes, Cookies, Breads, and More

Danielle Cochran

FAIR WINDS

Contents

Introduction ✳ **6**

Chapter 1: Kitchen Essentials ✳ **8**

Chapter 2: Cookies and Bars ✳ **20**

Chapter 3: Cakes and Cupcakes ✳ **46**

Chapter 4: Cheesecakes, Puddings, and Custards ✳ **72**

Chapter 5: Pies, Tarts, and Pastries ✳ **96**

Chapter 6: Sweet Breads, Muffins, and Rolls ✳ **116**

Chapter 7: Savory Breads ✳ **142**

Resources ✳ **171**

Acknowledgments ✳ **172**

About the Author ✳ **172**

Index ✳ **173**

Introduction

Welcome to my world of *Craveworthy Baking*! I'm Danielle, or as some know me, the Salty Cooker. In this cookbook, I'm thrilled to share something that's been a true labor of love: dozens of baking recipes that are free of gluten and dairy. That's right and just as delicious as the classic way they're made!

Baking is more than a passion for me. It's a journey of joy and creativity. I've tried to make every recipe in this book as enjoyable and straightforward as possible. I've broken down the steps and whenever I could, I've used single flours like 1:1 gluten-free flour or gluten-free bread flour to keep things simple, practical, and cost-effective.

In these pages, you'll discover a wonderful mix of timeless classics, like Chocolate Cake Every Which Way (page 69) and Chocolate Chip Walnut Cookies (page 33), and some exciting new creations, such as the Champagne Swiss Roll (page 63) and Bananas Foster Cheesecake (page 83). And the best part is that every recipe in this cookbook has passed the ultimate test—the no-one-will-know-it's-gluten-and-dairy-free challenge.

As you dive into these recipes, I'll be right there with you, sharing tips and tricks to make sure your baked goods turn out just right. And if you're feeling adventurous, I'll guide you on how to modify these recipes to create something uniquely yours.

But the most beautiful thing about these recipes is their flexibility. Whether you're gluten-free, dairy-free, or neither, you can enjoy these recipes in their traditional forms by using full gluten and/ or full dairy ingredients. This cookbook isn't just a collection of recipes; it's an invitation to explore the world of craveworthy baking, whether you have dietary preferences or simply a deep love for the taste of delicious baked goods. It's from my heart to your kitchen, and I hope you find as much joy in baking these treats as I have in creating them.

A Word from Danielle

My culinary journey began in Michigan, but life's adventures eventually led me to a cozy corner just outside of Wilmington, North Carolina. Here, I live with my husband, Joe, and our two dogs, Stitch and Tank.

Cooking wasn't always a part of my life. In fact, I used to joke that I'd marry a chef to satisfy my deep love for food while avoiding the kitchen. The turning point came around the age of 16 when I was living on my own: I dropped out of school and needed to eat. It was then that I started to experiment with cooking here and there.

After relocating to northern Michigan with Joe, we found ourselves in a place that was a bit isolated, with limited dining options. This is when the Food Network became my source of inspiration. I loved watching chefs like Ina Garten, Tyler Florence, and Emeril Lagasse. They became my culinary heroes. To learn more about cooking techniques, I purchased *The Professional Chef*, a book commonly used in culinary schools. I wanted to learn about proper techniques.

Yes, I started with straightforward cooking and grilling, long before I became known for my baking. I always aimed to be a well-rounded cook, exploring various aspects of the culinary world. The truth is, though, I'm ADHD—and so I get bored with one style of cooking! I like to keep things fun and go on different cooking kicks often.

A significant turning point came when a friend suggested I try a gluten- and dairy-free diet due to health issues I was experiencing, like headaches and stomach problems. The 30-day challenge I undertook was life-changing. I felt more energetic, had no more headaches, and my stomach issues disappeared.

During this time, I was blown away by the lack of gluten- and dairy-free options that retained the comforting flavors of traditional dishes. During those 30 days, I had constant cravings for the foods I was used to. So, I decided to experiment in the kitchen, developing recipes that were both gluten- and dairy-free. It was a path filled with trial and error and lots of hissy fits! I think this was when my dogs learned I swore in the kitchen. I dropped something so they would come running in to clean up! Best cleanup crew around! But my mission was clear: to re-create our favorite desserts and baked goods in such a way that no one could tell they were gluten- and dairy-free.

I'd taste each creation, and if I thought it was good, I'd offer samples to neighbors, friends, and family, withholding the information that everything was gluten- and dairy-free. After a few rounds of positive feedback, I realized I was onto something special. It was possible to re-create our favorite baked goods without gluten and dairy.

Because my journey began with traditional baking, using full gluten and dairy, all my recipes can be made gluten-free, dairy-free, or with the full gluten and dairy ingredients. To this day, every recipe I share on social media and in my blog must pass the test: "No one will know this is gluten-free and dairy-free."

I appreciate your support in purchasing my cookbook. Scan the QR code for exclusive baking videos featuring a handful of my favorite recipes from the book. Let's have fun baking together!

CHAPTER 1

Kitchen Essentials

The World of Baking and Universal Measuring ✳ 10

Baking and Kitchen Essentials ✳ 12

Emergency Baking Substitutions ✳ 13

Dairy-Free and Gluten-Free Guide ✳ 15

A Few Tips and Tricks ✳ 17

The World of Baking and Universal Measuring

Cooking and baking bring people together from all corners of the world, and when it comes to measurements, there are a variety of methods to choose from. Some enjoy the charm of using teaspoons, while others find precision in the trusty kitchen scale.

What's wonderful is that there's no one-size-fits-all answer here; it's all about your personal taste and what feels right for you. The joy of baking transcends borders and cultures, and it's perfectly okay to choose the method that makes your culinary journey as simple and enjoyable as possible.

So, whether you're whipping up a dessert in Australia or baking in Montreal, embrace your unique style and create mouthwatering delights that resonate with your heart and taste buds.

Below, I've crafted some charts with the hope of making the baking process more straightforward and enjoyable for you. So, find the method that resonates with your style, and let's dive into the delightful world of creating scrumptious desserts.

VOLUME

Use liquid measuring cups or a kitchen scale for liquids.

For dry ingredients, use dry measuring cups, leveling off excess with a flat edge.

WEIGHT

Place your scale on a level surface for accurate measurements.

Tare the scale with the container on it before adding the ingredient to zero out the container weight.

TEMPERATURE

Invest in an oven thermometer for accurate oven temperature readings.

Allow ingredients to reach room temperature before measuring for more accurate results.

LET'S FIGURE OUT SOME LIQUID MEASUREMENTS

Although different ingredients have slightly different weights, here are some general conversions you can use for U.S. and metric liquid measurement equivalents.

1 teaspoon = 5 ml	1/3 cup = 80 ml	1 cup = 235 ml
1 tablespoon = 15 ml	1/2 cup = 120 ml	1 pint = 475 ml
1 fluid ounce = 28 ml	2/3 cup = 160 ml	1 quart = 945 ml
1/4 cup = 60 ml	3/4 cup = 175 ml	1 gallon = 3.8 liters

LET'S TALK ABOUT WEIGHT

Here are some approximate conversions you can use for U.S. and metric weight measurement equivalents.

1 ounce = 28 g

2 ounces = 55 g

3 ounces = 85 g

4 ounces = 115 g

5 ounces = 140 g

6 ounces = 170 g

8 ounces = 225 g

12 ounces = 340 g

14 ounces = 395 g

1 pound = 455 g

ARE YOU FEELING HOT?

If you ever wondered how to convert your oven temperatures between U.S. and metric measurements, here you go!

NOTE: that the temperatures throughout the book are for standard ovens, so if you're using convection, reduce the temperature by 25 degrees Fahrenheit (°F).

275°F = 140°C

300°F = 150°C

325°F = 170°C

350°F = 180°C

375°F = 190°C

400°F = 200°C

425°F = 220°C

450°F = 230°C

475°F = 240°C

GO BANANAS!

Here's a handy guide to convert whole bananas into cup measurements.

½ banana = ⅓ cup (50 g) chopped or ¼ cup (56 g) mashed

1 banana = ⅔ cup (100 g) chopped or ½ cup (113 g) mashed

1½ bananas = 1 cup (150 g) chopped or ¾ cup (169 g) mashed

2 bananas = 1⅓ cups (200 g) chopped or 1 cup (225 g) mashed

3 bananas = 2 cups (300 g) chopped or 1½ cups (338 g) mashed

4 bananas = 2⅔ cups (400 g) chopped or 2 cups (450 g) mashed

Baking and Kitchen Essentials

I am excited to share the tools and equipment that have become my trusted companions on countless baking journeys. Before diving into a recipe, I make it a habit to sit down, carefully read through the recipe, and gather the items needed. This preparation sets the stage for a seamless and enjoyable baking experience. It's so convenient and allows less opportunity for error when I prepare this way. Hopefully you find it helpful too, though of course you will not need all of this for every recipe.

PREPARING, MIXING, MEASURING, AND SERVING

Kitchen scale	Grater box	Rolling pin
Measuring spoons	Safety glove (for grating)	Candy thermometer
Measuring cups	Mixing bowls	Kitchen thermometer
Sifter	Mini prep bowls	Oven mitts
Can opener	Silicone spatula	Toothpicks
Cutting boards	Wooden spoons	Pastry brush
Paring knife	Whisk	Timer
Sharp, large knife	Slotted spoon	Cooling racks
Bread cutting knife	Pastry blender	Frosting spatula
Cake knife	Bench knife	Piping bag and tips
Peeler	Various sizes cookie scoops	Pie spatula
Zester	Biscuit cutter	Airtight containers

BAKING AND COOKING

Baking sheets

Bundt pans

Deep baking dishes (2 to 4 inches [5 to 10 cm] deep)

Cookie sheets

Parchment paper

Skillets

Saucepan

Ramekins

Kitchen blowtorch

Cake pans

Muffin tin

Pie dish

Tart dish

Angel food pan

Silicone baking mats

Cupcake liners

EQUIPMENT

Blender

Food processor

Stand mixer or hand mixer

Dough rising pad

Emergency Baking Substitutions

LIQUID INGREDIENTS

Almond extract: Vanilla extract

Buttermilk: 1 cup (235 ml) = 1 cup (230 g) dairy-free plain yogurt (not Greek) or 1 cup (235 ml) oat or pea-protein milk + 1 tablespoon (15 ml) white vinegar or lemon juice; let the mixture sit until curdled before using, about 5 to 10 minutes

Heavy cream: 1 cup (235 ml) = 1 cup (235 ml) dairy-free whole milk + 1 tablespoon (14 g) vegetable or canola butter, melted

Lemon juice: 1 teaspoon (5 ml) = ½ teaspoon (2.5 ml) apple cider vinegar

Light brown sugar: 1 packed cup (225 g) = 1 cup (200 g) granulated sugar + 1 tablespoon (20 g) molasses, or 1 unpacked cup (150 g) dark brown sugar

Sour cream: 1 cup (230 g) = 1 cup (230 g) dairy-free plain yogurt

Vanilla extract: 1 teaspoon (5 ml) = 1 teaspoon (5 ml) bourbon or rum

Whole milk: 1 cup (235 ml) = 1 cup (235 ml) dairy-free skim or low-fat milk + 2 tablespoons (28 g) vegetable or canola butter, melted

Yogurt: 1 cup (230 g) = 1 cup (230 g) dairy-free sour cream

POWDERED INGREDIENTS

Baking powder: 1 teaspoon (4.6 g) = ½ teaspoon (2 g) cream of tartar + ¼ teaspoon (1.2 g) baking soda

Baking soda: ¼ teaspoon (1.2 g) = 1 teaspoon (4.6 g) baking powder

Cocoa powder: ½ cup (40 g) = ½ cup (40 g) Dutch process cocoa + replace the baking soda in the recipe with twice the amount of baking powder

Powdered sugar: 1 cup (120 g) = 1 cup (200 g) granulated sugar + 1 teaspoon (3 g) cornstarch ground in a blender

Dutch process cocoa powder: ½ cup (40 g) = ½ cup (40 g) natural cocoa + replace the baking powder in the recipe with half the amount of baking soda

Gluten-free flour: 1 cup (148 g) = 1 cup (125 g) all-purpose flour

Kosher salt: I use Morton's kosher salt. 1 teaspoon (6 g) of iodized table salt = 1¼ (7.5 g) teaspoon Morton's kosher salt = 2 teaspoons (6 g) Diamond Crystal kosher salt

Pumpkin pie spice: 1 teaspoon = ½ teaspoon (1 g) ground cinnamon + ¼ teaspoon (0.5 g) ground ginger + ⅛ teaspoon (0.3 g) ground clove + ⅛ teaspoon (0.3 g) freshly grated nutmeg

SOLID INGREDIENTS

Dried dates: Dried figs

Eggs: 1 egg = 3 tablespoons (42 g) mayonnaise, or 1 tablespoon (7 g) ground flaxseed + 3 tablespoons (45 ml) water; let sit 5 minutes before using. Exception: This substitution cannot be used for any recipes with egg whites.

Frostings: Store-bought frostings

Peanut butter: Sunflower butter, almond butter, or cashew butter

Pecans: Walnuts

Semisweet chocolate: 1 ounce (28 g) = 3 tablespoons (15 g) cocoa powder + 3 tablespoons (39 g) granulated sugar + 1 tablespoon oil (15 ml) or (14 g) vegetable or canola butter, melted

Walnuts: Pecans

Dairy-Free and Gluten-Free Guide

In this cookbook, I've done all the testing to make sure the recipes work dairy- and gluten-free. While I encourage flexibility, your product choices can affect recipes. In the section that follows, I'll share my go-to substitutes to facilitate a smooth transition between different products. Although each ingredient isn't identical, these suggestions aim to support you in successfully creating my recipes with confidence and ease.

DAIRY-FREE MILKS, BUTTERS, AND MORE

Milk

When it comes to dairy-free milk, I always prefer the thicker options, like creamy oat milk or pea-protein milk. They're simply better at mimicking regular milk when baking and will give you the best results. My personal favorite is pea-protein milk, hands down, for its consistency and taste resemblance to regular milk. Now, if you have another favorite milk and you want to sub it in, that is up to you. The only thing I'll caution against is almond milk, unless I've specifically mentioned it for a recipe. Almond milk is essentially water, and will not provide the best-quality baked goods. You want something heartier to create a moist, flavorful baked good. We're trying to mimic dairy milk as much as possible.

*

Butter

While there's a range of dairy-free butter alternatives available, they don't all perform the same in recipes. I have experimented with different types over the years to see what works best. My go-to recommendations are butter-like sticks made with vegetable oil, canola oil, or avocado oil (unless a different kind is specified). Again, if you have your own favorites, feel free to experiment, but know that recipes may turn out differently. For example, using olive oil–based butter will generally give your baked goods a crunchier crust and a denser texture, which can be okay or not depending on the recipe. Note that if dairy-free butter isn't required for your diet, in most cases, regular butter can be swapped in unless I've specified otherwise.

Other Dairy

Other dairy-free products come in more dramatically different formulations and I've found it can really affect baking times. Take dairy-free cream cheese, for instance: some might turn more liquidy when baked, messing with the baking times. But I've put a lot of batches through the oven to figure out the differences in timing using various brands. So, when recipes feature these ingredients, you might notice variations of up to 10 to 15 minutes in some recipes. Be sure to read the recipe in its entirely on what to look for to know when your baked item is good to go. There simply was no better way to handle this, as I couldn't make the book work for all readers in all locations if I mandated using a specific brand.

GLUTEN-FREE FLOURS

Using great-quality gluten-free flour is like the secret sauce in these recipes. Each flour I mention for a specific recipe has been carefully chosen for its perfect match. Swapping one flour type for another, like going from a 1-to-1 gluten-free flour to cassava flour, not only changes the taste, but also the texture, bake time, and overall flavor profile of a baked good. To keep things tasting just right, I highly recommend sticking to the specific flour I suggest in the recipes. As a general note, I highly recommend Caputo Gluten-Free bread flour for all bread flour recipes.

CONVERTING TO FULL GLUTEN OR FULL DAIRY

Converting these recipes from gluten-free to gluten-containing flours is pretty simple: there's no math needed! Just swap out the gluten-free flour for all-purpose or bread flour, depending on the recipe, and you're good to go. You might notice a slight variation in baking times, around 5 to 8 minutes on average. Just use the same advice listed to check for that perfect doneness.

Similarly, turning recipes from dairy-free to full dairy products is easy—no measurements need tweaking. But using regular dairy can affect baking times by about 5 to 8 minutes as well. You'll just need to pay more attention to sensory cues.

A Few Tips and Tricks

EVERYTHING

These are the ultimate tips—they apply to everything you're baking!

Scraping: Be sure to scrape down the bowl and beaters while mixing to ensure that all the ingredients are thoroughly incorporated.

Butter temperature: Pay attention to the butter's temperature as specified in the recipe; melted, cold, and room temperature butter can yield different results in both flavor and texture.

Egg temperature: Unless the recipe specifies otherwise or when whipping egg whites, using room temperature eggs is generally best for baking.

COOKIES

I have such a love for cookies, and over the years, through experimentation and learning, I've uncovered some invaluable tips and tricks that consistently yield fabulous results.

Mixer attachment: When making cookies, particularly if you're using a stand mixer, opt for a whisk or paddle attachment for the best results.

Creaming butter and sugar: For perfect cookies, beat sugar and room-temperature butter for about 5 minutes or until the mixture transforms into a light and fluffy consistency.

Incorporating dry ingredients: When adding dry ingredients to your cookie dough, start the mixer at a slow speed, gradually increasing it to efficiently work in the flour. Mix until just combined—avoid overmixing. When uncertain, finish mixing by hand using a spatula.

Storage: The best way to store your cookies is in an airtight container.

Preheating: Preheating the oven is important for all baking and baking times. Make sure your oven is completely preheated before baking, and place a rack in the center of the oven.

Prep cookie sheets: Prepare the cookie sheets in advance, so everything is ready to go once your cookie dough is ready.

Cool pans: Avoid placing cookie dough on hot pans; let the pans cool down a bit before baking.

Cool cookies: Allow the cookies to cool completely on a wire rack after baking.

Scoop: When making cookies, using a cookie scoop is a great way to ensure they are uniform in size, leading to consistent baking times.

Rotate for evenness: Halfway through baking, rotate the cookie sheet or baking dish to ensure an even bake.

Freezing: Wondering if you can freeze cookie dough? Absolutely! I love freezing leftovers and mixing two doughs for a unique cookie. Just wrap it well, and it can be frozen for up to 3 months. Remember to let it thaw before baking.

YEAST BREAD

Gluten-free bread has been a real challenge for me over the years. However, by following the tips below, you can overcome the challenges and achieve gluten-free bread success, just as I have. In this book, dry instant yeast is used (2¼ teaspoons or 1 packet [9 g]).

Mixer attachment: When using a stand mixer for bread, the paddle attachment is ideal.

Yeast activation: Most yeast bread recipes in this book have the yeast activation as a separate part in the recipe. This is done on purpose to make sure the yeast activates before adding it to the bread mixture. This is the most common mistake in making yeasted bread. If the temperature of the water is incorrect, the yeast does not activate. Warm water that is 110°F (43°C) or close to it is a must for this process to happen. If your yeast does not activate within 5 minutes to create a thick foamy head, start this process over again.

Proper rising: Place yeast doughs in a draft-free area to allow them to rise effectively.

Plastic wrap: When a recipe calls for using plastic wrap, a handy tip is to apply nonstick cooking spray to the side of the wrap that will be in contact with the dough. This prevents the dough from sticking to the wrap.

Cooling for flavor: Gluten-free yeasted breads taste best when cooled. They retain moisture, and as they cool, this moisture is released. It can be challenging to remember this with a tempting warm loaf.

No make-ahead: Yeasted doughs, especially gluten- and dairy-free ones, cannot be made in advance, frozen, or stored in the fridge, as it affects the rise, texture, and taste.

CAKES

Cakes are the ultimate treat for celebrations. With a couple of tips, you can ensure your cake turns out perfectly, ready to be the centerpiece of your next celebration.

Mixer attachment: When mixing cake batter, particularly in a stand mixer, choose the whisk attachment for best results.

Oven care: While baking a cake, avoid slamming the oven door, and be mindful of other doors in the house as well. Sudden door slamming can cause a cake to collapse.

Sift: For the best results, sift the dry ingredients together before adding to the wet mixture.

Cooling grace period: After the cake is done baking, let it rest in the pan for about 10 minutes before gently flipping it onto a cooling rack. This allows the cake to settle and maintain its structure.

Trimming: Some cakes are best trimmed. This means removing the edges and leveling the top if it is too domed.

Flattening: If your cake is domed and you are making a double-layer cake, once the cake is partially cooled in the pan, flip it upside down on a wire cooling rack. This can help flatten the dome.

Frosting: Always let a cake cool completely before frosting. Start by adding a crumb layer of frosting. This is a thin layer of frosting all around the cake that traps the crumbs in place. Then, add the final thicker layer of frosting. It will be crumb-free.

Perfect whipped egg whites: Keep the beaters and bowl clean and grease-free. Egg whites are best cold. Be careful not to overbeat. When you hit soft peaks, reduce the speed to medium until stiff peaks are formed (the egg white should stand on its own).

Freezing: Can I freeze the cake? The cake itself can be baked, cooled completely, wrapped tightly in plastic wrap, and stored in the freezer for 1 month. Allow it to come to room temperature before adding frosting.

QUICK BREADS

Work quickly: Handle the dough with care. Work quickly to avoid overworking the dough and to keep the butter cold. Keeping the butter as cold as possible is key. When in doubt, place the mixture in the fridge or freezer for 10 to 20 minutes to keep the butter cold. Cutting in the butter quickly is also crucial for producing a nice light biscuit.

CHEESECAKES AND PUDDINGS

Cream cheese temperature: Room temperature cream cheese is key to assure the texture turns out properly.

Mixing: Be careful not to overmix your cream cheese mixture. This will result in a different texture cheesecake.

Pudding/custard temperature: Have all ingredients at room temperature before baking. This will prevent the eggs from scrambling during the baking process.

PIES AND TARTS

Pie filling: For fruit-based pies, cooking down the pie filling on the stove beforehand will prevent a soupy pie. Make sure it is room temperature or cold before using.

Crust temperature: Keep the pie crust nice and cold. This will result in a flakey crust.

Golden brown: Bake pies until they are nice and golden brown. For a double pie crust recipe, to achieve that golden crust, I like to brush the top with an egg wash and sprinkle a little sugar on top.

Cooling: Cool pies completely before cutting. They need time to set up.

Freezing: Can I freeze pie crust? Yes, you can. Wrap it tightly in plastic wrap and it can be stored in the freezer for 3 months. Then bring to slightly above room temperature before using it.

CHAPTER 2

Cookies and Bars

Chocolate Caramel Revel Bars ✳ 23

Cherry Hazelnut Biscotti ✳ 24

Classic Apple Oatmeal Cookies ✳ 27

Snickerdoodle Cookies ✳ 28

Banana Bread Cookies ✳ 30

Chocolate Chip Walnut Cookies ✳ 33

Peanut Butter and Jelly Oatmeal Bars ✳ 34

Strawberry Shortcake Blondie Bars ✳ 37

Gooey S'mores Brownies ✳ 38

Turtle Chocolate Chip Skillet Cookie ✳ 41

Peanut Butter Cookie Sandwiches ✳ 42

Lemon Bars ✳ 45

Chocolate Caramel Revel Bars

Oh, revel bars, how I love you! The first time I ever had one, I was around ten years old and living in rural Michigan. All our neighbors were Amish. Anytime they would come over to use the phone, the next day they would bring us a freshly baked treat. Everything they baked was phenomenal. One day, the treat was a batch of revel bars. To this day I have a tough time controlling myself around these bad boys!

Yield: 12 bars, one 9 x 13-inch (23 x 33-cm) baking dish

FOR THE DOUGH:

1½ cups (340 g) packed light brown sugar

1 cup (225 g) vegetable or canola butter, room temperature

2 eggs

2 cups (296 g) 1:1 gluten-free flour

3 cups (270 g) gluten-free rolled oats

1 teaspoon (4.6 g) baking soda

½ teaspoon (2.3 g) baking powder

1½ teaspoons (7.5 ml) vanilla extract

FOR THE TOPPING:

¾ cup (131 g) dairy-free dark chocolate chips

¾ cup (131 g) dairy-free semisweet chocolate chips

1 can (14 ounces or 395 g) dairy-free sweetened condensed milk

2 tablespoons (28 g) vegetable or canola butter

To make the dough:

1. Place an oven rack in the center position. Preheat the oven to 350°F (180°C) and spray nonstick spray in a 9 x 13-inch (23 x 33-cm) baking dish.

2. In a large bowl, using a mixer fitted with a whisk or paddle, add the brown sugar and butter and mix on high for 3 minutes. After mixing, add the eggs and mix for another 3 minutes. Turn off your mixer, add the remaining dough ingredients, and mix on medium for another 3 to 5 minutes.

To make the topping:

1. In a medium saucepan, add the ingredients and cook over low heat until melted and blended. Once melted and well incorporated, remove from heat.

2. Press three-quarters of the bar mixture into the bottom of your greased baking dish. Next, spread the melted chocolate mixture evenly on top of your pressed bar mixture. Add the remaining bar mixture on top of the chocolate. It is a crumble; it will not cover everything.

3. Bake for 20 to 30 minutes until the top turns a light golden brown. The center will still jiggle. You want it to cool completely in the dish before cutting them into squares.

Cherry Hazelnut Biscotti

I've always had a great relationship with my mother-in-law, Vicky, and once a year we would do a food tour/class together. One year, she signed us up for a bruschetta class. We were so excited. When we arrived, we were both shocked—it was a biscotti class. We're both dyslexic and were dying laughing! So, that day we took a class on how to make biscotti!

Yield: 36 biscotti

3 eggs, divided

¾ cup (150 g) granulated sugar

¾ cup (170 g) packed light brown sugar

¾ cup + 1 tablespoon (179 g) vegetable or canola butter, room temperature

2 teaspoons (10 ml) vanilla extract

3 cups (444 g) 1:1 gluten-free flour

1 cup (104 g) almond flour

½ teaspoon (3 g) kosher salt (Morton's)

2 teaspoons (9.2 g) baking powder

1 cup (160 g) dried cherries

1 cup (115 g) hazelnuts, chopped

1 tablespoon (15 ml) water

2 tablespoons (26 g) raw sugar, divided

VARIATION

❊ Try melting some dark chocolate to drizzle over or dip the ends of the biscotti. Ensure the biscotti are fully cooled first.

1. Place an oven rack in the center position. Preheat the oven to 300°F (150°C) and prepare a large baking sheet with parchment paper.

2. In a small bowl, separate one egg white.

3. With mixer off and a whisk attached, add both sugars and the butter to the bowl. Turn the mixer to high and beat for 3 minutes. Reduce speed to low and add the vanilla and the 2 whole eggs and extra yolk. Blend on medium speed for 3 minutes until the mixture is light and fluffy. Add the flours, salt, and baking powder with the mixer off. Mix on medium just until incorporated; avoid overmixing. Scrape down the sides. Fold in the cherries and hazelnuts.

4. Transfer the dough to a lightly floured surface, forming it into two logs about 10 inches (25 cm) long and 2 inches (5 cm) in diameter. Place onto the lined baking sheet.

5. Add water to the reserved egg white, mix well, and brush onto the top of the biscotti logs. Sprinkle 1 tablespoon (13 g) of the raw sugar over the biscotti logs. Set aside the egg wash.

6. Bake on the middle oven rack for 45 minutes. Allow the partially baked biscotti to rest for 30 minutes.

7. For the second baking phase, line two cookie sheets with parchment paper. Reduce the oven temperature to 275°F (140°C).

8. Use a serrated knife to cut the biscotti logs into individual slices, each ½- to ¾-inch (1- to 2-cm) thick. Place on the lined cookie sheets with minimal spacing. Apply the egg wash mixture to each piece, and sprinkle the remaining raw sugar. Bake each cookie sheet separately for 45 minutes or until the biscotti are firm and golden. Let them cool on the sheet before removing.

Classic Apple Oatmeal Cookies

Who doesn't love classic oatmeal cookies? This recipe serves as an excellent base recipe, allowing you to have endless flavor possibilities. Pro tip for ultimate oatmeal cookies: Let the dough rest overnight, tightly wrapped in the fridge. This simple step allows the flavors to come together and the oatmeal to soften, resulting in cookies that are simply soft and delicious.

Yield: 20 cookies

1 cup (225 g) vegetable or canola butter, room temperature

1 cup (225 g) packed light brown sugar

⅓ cup (67 g) granulated sugar

2 eggs

2 teaspoons (10 ml) vanilla extract

1¾ cups (259 g) 1:1 gluten-free flour

2½ cups (360 g) gluten-free old-fashioned oats

1 teaspoon (6 g) kosher salt (Morton's)

1 teaspoon (4.6 g) baking soda

½ teaspoon (2.3 g) baking powder

1¼ teaspoons (3 g) ground cinnamon

⅛ teaspoon (0.3 g) nutmeg

⅛ teaspoon (0.2 g) allspice

1 cup (150 g) peeled, cored, and finely diced or grated apple

1. In a stand mixer with whisk and medium bowl, add the butter and sugars. Mix on high speed for 5 minutes until light and fluffy. Mix in the eggs, one at a time, ensuring each egg is fully incorporated. Stir in the vanilla. Gradually add the flour, oats, salt, baking soda, baking powder, cinnamon, nutmeg, and allspice. Mix until just incorporated. Fold in the apple.

2. Wrap the dough in plastic wrap and place it in the refrigerator overnight.

3. Place an oven rack in the center position. Preheat the oven to 350°F (180°C) and line 2 cookie sheets with parchment paper. Using a 2-tablespoon (30-ml) cookie scoop, scoop equal-size portions of cookie dough onto the prepared cookie sheets, leaving 2 inches (5 cm) of space between each cookie. Bake the cookies for 12 to 14 minutes or until the edges turn golden brown and the tops are lightly browned. Remove the cookies from the oven and allow them to cool completely on the cookie sheet.

Snickerdoodle Cookies

I was so surprised by the results of my Instagram poll on everyone's favorite cookie! It turns out that snickerdoodles stole the show and claimed the number one spot, leaving even classic chocolate chip cookies in the dust. I would have bet my money on chocolate chip, but the power of snickerdoodles won! Here is my best version of the favored snickerdoodle.

Yield: 30 cookies

FOR THE DOUGH:

1¹⁄₃ cups (267 g) granulated sugar

1 cup (225 g) vegetable or canola butter, room temperature

2 eggs

2 teaspoons (10 ml) vanilla extract

2½ cups (370 g) 1:1 gluten-free flour

¾ teaspoon (4.5 g) kosher salt (Morton's)

2 teaspoons (7 g) cream of tartar

1½ teaspoons (6.9 g) baking soda

FOR THE COATING:

½ cup (100 g) granulated sugar

1 tablespoon (7 g) ground cinnamon

To make the dough:

1. Place an oven rack in the center position. Preheat the oven to 350°F (180°C) and line 3 cookie sheets with parchment paper.

2. In a stand mixer with a whisk and a large mixing bowl, combine the sugar and butter. Mix on high speed for 5 minutes until light and creamy. Make sure to scrape down the sides of the bowl to ensure even mixing. Add the eggs one at a time, mixing well after each addition. Then, mix in the vanilla. Gradually add the flour, salt, cream of tartar, and baking soda. Mix on high speed until the dry ingredients are just incorporated.

To make the coating:

1. In a separate small mixing bowl, combine the sugar and cinnamon for the sugar coating, mixing well.

2. Use a 2-tablespoon (30-ml) cookie scoop to scoop equal-size portions of cookie dough. Roll each portion into a ball, then coat the dough balls in the sugar-cinnamon mixture until fully coated. Place the coated dough balls onto the prepared cookie sheets, leaving about 2 inches (5 cm) of space between each cookie.

3. Bake the cookies in the preheated oven for 10 to 12 minutes. The tops of the cookies should not appear shiny, and the edges should be barely golden brown. Once baked, remove the cookies from the oven and allow them to cool for 5 minutes before putting them on a wire rack.

NOTE

❊ These cookies can be stored in an airtight container for several days to maintain freshness.

Banana Bread Cookies

During the process of testing the recipes for this book, I had dozens of people try these cookies, along with several other recipes. This is one of the few recipes where there just was no debate. Anyone that tried these loved them! Give these a try to see if they will become your new favorite cookies.

Yield: 20 cookies

FOR THE DOUGH:

3¼ cups (481 g) 1:1 gluten-free flour

1½ tablespoons (12 g) cornstarch

1½ teaspoons (6.9 g) baking powder

½ teaspoon (2.3 g) baking soda

1 teaspoon (6 g) kosher salt (Morton's)

1 teaspoon (2 g) ground cinnamon

¼ teaspoon (0.5 g) allspice

1 cup (225 g) vegetable or canola butter, room temperature

1 cup (225 g) packed light brown sugar

½ cup (100 g) granulated sugar

1 cup (225 g) mashed banana (about 2 large bananas)

1 egg

2 teaspoons (10 ml) vanilla extract

1 cup (120 g) chopped walnuts

FOR THE FROSTING:

8 ounces (225 g) dairy-free cream cheese, room temperature

2 tablespoons (28 g) vegetable or canola butter, room temperature

1½ cups (180 g) powdered sugar

1 teaspoon (5 ml) vanilla extract

½ cup (60 g) chopped walnuts

To make the dough:

1. Place an oven rack in the center position. Preheat the oven to 350°F (180°C). Line 2 cookie sheets with parchment paper.

2. In a medium mixing bowl, whisk together the flour, cornstarch, baking powder, baking soda, salt, cinnamon, and allspice. Mix until combined.

3. In a separate large mixing bowl, cream together the butter and sugars using an electric mixer on high speed for about 5 minutes or until light and fluffy. Mix in the banana, egg, and vanilla until well incorporated. Gradually add the dry ingredients to the bowl, mixing until just combined. Gently fold in the walnuts.

4. Using a 3-tablespoon (45 ml) cookie scoop or spoon, drop equal-size portions of cookie dough onto the parchment-lined cookie sheets, spacing them 2 inches (5 cm) apart. Bake the cookies for 12 to 14 minutes until lightly golden brown. Remove from the oven and allow to cool on the cookie sheet for 1 hour before removing to a wire rack to finish cooling.

To make the frosting:

1. In a mixing bowl, mix the cream cheese, butter, powdered sugar, and vanilla until smooth and creamy. Top each cooled cookie with a dollop of frosting and sprinkle chopped walnuts on top.

Chocolate Chip Walnut Cookies

It's hard to beat a good chocolate chip cookie. This cookie is pretty traditional, but you can transform it to your liking. While I love walnuts, you can easily switch up the nut to your preferred choice or omit and add more chocolate. The chocolate chips can be swapped for white chocolate. Play around and have some fun! There are so many options. Want one big cookie cake? Spread this cookie dough out in a skillet for a large cookie treat.

Yield: 12 cookies

½ cup (112 g) vegetable or canola butter, room temperature

½ cup (115g) packed light brown sugar

⅓ cup (67 g) granulated sugar

1 egg

1½ teaspoons (7.5 ml) vanilla extract

1½ cups (222 g) 1:1 gluten-free flour

2 teaspoons (6 g) arrowroot powder or cornstarch

1 teaspoon (4.6 g) baking soda

1 cup (175 g) dairy-free semisweet chocolate chips

1 cup (175 g) dairy-free bittersweet chocolate chips

1 cup (120 g) chopped walnuts

1. Using a stand mixer with a paddle attachment, add butter and both sugars. Turn your mixer on medium/high and mix for 5 minutes or until light and a little fluffy. Switch to low and add the egg and vanilla to the bowl. Mix until incorporated. Turn your mixer off and scrape the sides.

2. In a separate medium bowl, sift the flour, arrowroot powder, and baking soda together. Add slowly on medium speed and mix until combined. Don't overmix. Gently fold chocolate and walnuts into the dough. Put your dough in the refrigerator for at least 6 hours.

3. Place an oven rack in the center position. Preheat the oven to 350°F (180°C) and line 2 baking sheets with parchment paper. Using a 2-tablespoon (30 ml) cookie scoop, scoop equal 1½-inch (4 cm) scoops to ensure even baking. Bake your cookies for 10 to 13 minutes on the middle rack. Cookies should be lightly golden brown. Allow your cookies to cool completely on your baking sheet before moving.

NOTES

✳ If time permits, allow your dough to chill for 24 hours in the refrigerator. Chilled dough bakes the best.

✳ At the 10-minute mark of baking, the outside of the cookie will be slightly crispy, and the inside will be gooey. The longer you bake it, the more it will crisp.

Peanut Butter and Jelly Oatmeal Bars

It's peanut butter jelly time! I admit, this flavor combination was a total last-minute experiment when making these oatmeal bars for the cookbook, but now I won't make them any other way. After shooting the photographs you see here, I ate half the pan myself. They are irresistible.

Yield: 6 bars, one 8 x 8-inch (20 x 20-cm) baking dish

FOR THE JAM:

2 cups (510 g) frozen strawberries

2 tablespoons (26 g) granulated sugar

¼ cup (60 ml) water

2 tablespoons (16 g) cornstarch

FOR THE DOUGH:

1⅓ cups (197 g) 1:1 gluten-free flour

1½ cups (135 g) gluten-free rolled oats

¾ cup (170 g) packed light brown sugar

½ cup (112 g) vegetable or canola butter, melted and cooled

1½ teaspoons (7.5 ml) vanilla extract

FOR ASSEMBLY:

½ cup (130 g) creamy peanut butter

To make the jam:

1. In a small saucepan, combine the frozen strawberries, sugar, water, and cornstarch. Cook the mixture over medium heat, smashing the strawberries down as they cook. Continue cooking for 10 minutes over medium heat, then cook an additional 15 to 20 minutes on low until the mixture reaches a jamlike consistency. Set aside.

To make the dough:

1. Place an oven rack in the center position. Preheat the oven to 350°F (180°C) and grease an 8 x 8-inch (20 x 20-cm) baking dish with baking spray.

2. In a large mixing bowl, combine the oats, brown sugar, butter, and vanilla. Use a fork or pastry cutter to mix the ingredients until a crumbly texture forms.

To assemble:

1. Press two-thirds of the mixture into the bottom of the prepared baking dish.

2. Pour the previously prepared jam over the pressed mixture in an even layer. Add dollops of the creamy peanut butter and swirl around with a butter knife. Sprinkle the remaining dough mixture over top and bake in the preheated oven for 34 to 45 minutes or until the top turns golden brown.

3. Allow to cool completely before cutting into bars.

NOTE

✳ These bars can be stored in an airtight container for freshness.

Strawberry Shortcake Blondie Bars

Blondies are such a fun changeup when you want a gooey delicious treat, but just aren't feeling chocolate. This recipe can be modified, though, by adding chocolate chips for a compromise. Or try omitting or changing the fruit for new flavors.

Yield: 15 bars, one 9 x 13-inch (23 x 33-cm) baking dish

FOR THE BATTER:

1 cup (225 g) packed light brown sugar

⅓ cup (67 g) granulated sugar

1 cup (225 g) vegetable or canola butter, melted

3 eggs

2 teaspoons (10 ml) vanilla extract

2½ cups (370 g) 1:1 gluten-free flour

2 tablespoons (16 g) cornstarch

1 teaspoon (4.6 g) baking powder

¾ teaspoon (4.5 g) kosher salt (Morton's)

1½ cups (218 g) fresh strawberries, sliced

1 cup (175 g) dairy-free white chocolate chips

FOR THE GLAZE:

1½ cups (180 g) powdered sugar

1½ tablespoons (30 g) strawberry jam or puree

2 tablespoons (28 ml) water, divided

To make the batter:

1. Place an oven rack in the center position. Preheat the oven to 350°F (180°C). Spray a 9 x 13-inch (23 x 33-cm) baking dish with nonstick baking spray.

2. With a stand mixer with a whisk or paddle and a medium mixing bowl, mix both sugars and melted butter until light and fluffy. Add in the eggs and vanilla and mix until well combined. Scrape down the sides of the bowl and add the remaining ingredients. Mix until just incorporated, being careful not to overmix.

3. Pour into the prepared baking dish and bake for 25 to 30 minutes. This will look underbaked, but I promise, it will not be! It will firm up as it cools.

To make the glaze:

1. In a small mixing bowl, combine the powdered sugar and jam or puree until fully combined. Add 1 tablespoon (15 ml) of the water and mix. Depending on the consistency, you may need to add an additional tablespoon (15 ml) of water. We want this to have some thickness to it, but not to the point that you cannot drizzle it.

2. Once you have the desired consistency, drizzle over the cooled blondies to your liking.

✳

Gooey S'mores Brownies

It's a well-known fact I am obsessed with anything and everything s'mores. On social media I am often called the "s'mores queen" because I will turn everything into a s'more! The combo is one of my all-time favorites. It's gooey, Chocolatey (with a capital C), and simply delicious.

Yield: 9 servings, one 8 x 8-inch (20 x 20-cm) baking dish

FOR THE BATTER:

½ cup (112 g) vegetable or canola butter, room temperature

1⅓ cups (267 g) granulated sugar

2 eggs

1 teaspoon (2 g) espresso powder

1 tablespoon (15 ml) vanilla extract

¾ cup (60 g) cocoa powder

¾ cup (111 g) 1:1 gluten-free flour

½ teaspoon (3 g) kosher salt (Morton's)

1 cup (175 g) dairy-free dark chocolate chips

FOR ASSEMBLY:

4 large gluten-free graham crackers (should fit the entire bottom of the baking dish)

4 ounces (115 g) marshmallow fluff

To make the batter:

1. Place an oven rack in the center position. Preheat your oven to 350°F (180°C) and generously coat an 8 x 8-inch (20 x 20-cm) baking dish with nonstick baking spray.

2. In stand mixer with a medium bowl, whisk together butter and sugar for 3 minutes until the mixture becomes lighter in color. Incorporate eggs, followed by espresso powder and vanilla. Mix together on high for 3 minutes, ensuring a well-incorporated base. Scrape down the sides of the bowl. Gradually add the cocoa powder, flour, and salt, and mix until all items are blended. With a gentle hand, fold in the chocolate chips—we want these incorporated, but not beaten into the batter.

To assemble:

1. To create the layers in your prepared dish, start with a graham cracker foundation followed by a lavish pour of two-thirds of the brownie mixture. The batter is thick, so spread it evenly as best as you can. Dollop marshmallow fluff on top, spreading it ever-so-slightly. Finish the layers with the remaining brownie batter. There's no need for meticulous spreading; each scoop will find its place once baking.

2. Bake in the oven for 30 to 35 minutes. The center should exhibit a gentle jiggle to it when done. Remove from the oven and cool for 20 minutes before digging in.

Turtle Chocolate Chip Skillet Cookie

This cookie skillet is perfect for a get-together or family dinner night. Bake it in one large skillet and top with dairy-free ice cream, caramel, chocolate, and pecans. Have everyone grab a spoon and dig in!

Yield: 6 servings

1 can (11.25 ounces, or 320 g) dairy-free sweetened condensed milk

¾ cup (170 g) packed light brown sugar

½ cup (100 g) granulated sugar

1 cup (225 g) vegetable or canola butter, room temperature

1 tablespoon (15 ml) vanilla extract

2 eggs

2¼ cups (333 g) 1:1 gluten-free flour

1 teaspoon (4.6 g) baking soda

2½ teaspoons (11.5 g) baking powder

1 teaspoon (6 g) kosher salt (Morton's)

12 ounces (340 g) dairy-free chocolate chips (a mix of semisweet and dark chocolate)

⅓ cup (80 g) caramel

¼ cup (28 g) chopped pecans

1. Place an oven rack in the center position. Preheat the oven to 350°F (180°C). Spray a 12-inch (30-cm) cast-iron skillet with nonstick baking spray. Pour the sweetened condensed milk in the skillet and set aside.

2. In a mixer with a whisk attachment, combine the sugars and butter. Mix on high speed for 5 minutes until light and fluffy. Scrape down the sides of the bowl to ensure thorough mixing. Add the eggs one at a time, mixing well after each addition. Then, add the vanilla and mix for 3 minutes. Scrape down the sides of the bowl.

3. In a separate medium mixing bowl, whisk together the flour, baking soda, baking powder, and salt. Gradually add the dry ingredients to the first bowl. Mix until just incorporated, being careful not to overmix. Scrape down the sides of the bowl. Gently fold in the chocolate chips, incorporating them evenly.

4. Transfer the cookie dough into the prepared cast-iron skillet, spreading it out evenly with a flat mixing spatula. Bake the skillet cookie in the preheated oven for 22 to 26 minutes, depending on your desired texture. Closer to 22 minutes will result in a gooey base, while closer to 26 minutes will yield a crispier texture. Once baked to your liking, remove the skillet from the oven and let the cookie cool for a few minutes.

5. Serve this delectable chocolate chip cookie skillet warm, either on its own or with a scoop of dairy-free ice cream for an extra indulgence. Top with caramel and chopped pecans.

✳

Peanut Butter Cookie Sandwiches

There's something about a peanut butter cookie that hits the spot each time. They are the perfect combination of sweet and salty, and so satisfying. I love the simplicity of this recipe and that I can add hazelnut to take these cookies to another level. This is one of my favorite quick treats to make when I have a craving!

Yield: 14 cookies

FOR THE DOUGH:

½ cup + 1 tablespoon (126 g) vegetable or canola butter, room temperature

½ cup (115 g) packed light brown sugar

⅓ cup (67 g) granulated sugar

1 egg

2 teaspoons (10 ml) vanilla extract

¾ cup (195 g) crunchy peanut butter

1 cup (148 g) 1:1 gluten-free flour

¾ teaspoon (4.5 g) kosher salt (Morton's)

¾ teaspoon (3.45 g) baking soda

FOR ASSEMBLY:

½ cup (128 g) dairy-free hazelnut chocolate spread

½ cup (75 g) finely chopped peanuts

To make the dough:

1. Place an oven rack in the center position. Preheat the oven to 350°F (180°C) and line 2 cookie sheets with parchment paper.

2. In a stand mixer with a whisk attachment and medium bowl, add butter and sugars. Mix on high for 5 minutes or until light and fluffy. Add in the egg, vanilla, and peanut butter, and blend well. Scrape down the sides of the bowl. Add the flour, salt, and baking soda and mix for 1 minute or until just incorporated. Overmixing the dough will change the texture of the cookie.

3. Using a cookie scoop, scoop equal size cookies and place on the parchment-lined cookie sheets. Use a fork to press down gently to make a crisscross pattern.

4. Bake the cookies for 11 to 13 minutes or until the edges are slightly golden brown. Remove from the oven and allow to cool on the cookie sheet for 10 minutes. Transfer the cookies to a wire rack to cool completely.

To assemble:

1. Add hazelnut spread in between two cookies to create a sandwich. Roll the edges in the finely chopped peanuts.

Lemon Bars

These lemon bars are truly exceptional! Even though my husband and I aren't typically fans of lemon desserts, we can't resist devouring these. I think this is a perfect warm-weather dessert to pass around the table.

Yield: 24 bars, one 9 x 13-inch (23 x 33-cm) baking dish

FOR THE CRUST:

1 cup (225 g) vegetable or canola butter, melted

1/3 cup (67 g) granulated sugar

1¾ cups (259 g) 1:1 gluten-free flour

Pinch salt

1½ teaspoons (7.5 ml) vanilla extract

FOR THE FILLING:

1¼ cups (285 ml) lemon juice

2 tablespoons (12 g) lemon zest

1/2 cup (74 g) 1:1 gluten-free flour

1¾ cups (350 g) granulated sugar

6 eggs, room temperature

2 tablespoons (15 g) powdered sugar

NOTES

✳ If the parchment paper comes over the sides, it will be easier to remove the bars later.

✳ Store any leftover bars in an airtight container in the refrigerator for freshness.

To make the crust:

1. Place an oven rack in the center position. Preheat the oven to 350°F (180°C). Spray a 9 x 13-inch (23 x 33-cm) baking dish with nonstick baking spray and line it with parchment paper.

2. In a medium mixing bowl, combine all the ingredients for the crust. Mix well until everything is thoroughly combined and clumps together. Press the mixture firmly into the base of the prepared baking dish.

3. Bake the crust for 15 to 18 minutes until it turns lightly golden brown. Remove from the oven and reduce the oven temperature to 325°F (170°C).

To make the filling:

1. In a stand mixer with a paddle or whisk and a large mixing bowl, add lemon juice, lemon zest, flour, sugar, and eggs. Mix for 3 minutes on medium speed until well combined. Scrape down the sides.

2. Pour the filling over the crust in the baking dish and spread it evenly.

3. Bake the bars for 24 to 26 minutes until the edges turn slightly golden brown. Keep an eye on them so you don't overcook them! Remove the dish from the oven and let the bars sit at room temperature for 1 hour.

4. After the cool time, transfer to the refrigerator and let them set up for 6 hours. Run a sharp knife around the edges to separate the bars from the dish. These will be a little sticky.

5. Once fully set, dust the bars with powdered sugar for an elegant touch. When ready to serve, cut into 24 squares.

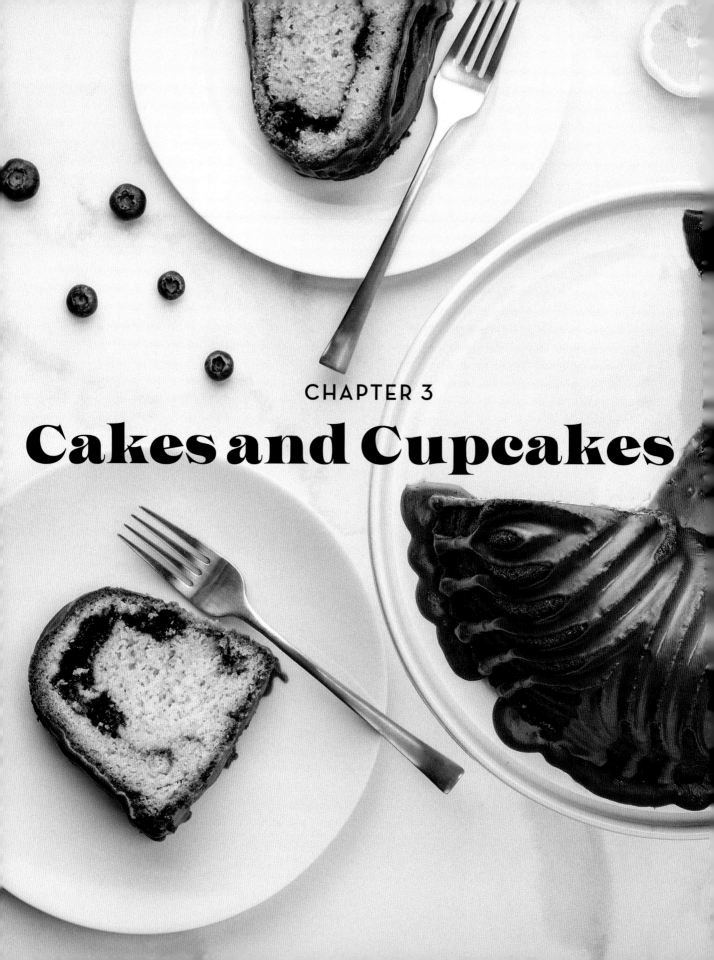

CHAPTER 3

Cakes and Cupcakes

Hummingbird Cake ✳ 49

Upside-Down Pineapple Cake ✳ 50

Chocolate Coconut Tres Leches Cake ✳ 53

Orange Creamsicle Cupcakes ✳ 54

Coconut Cake with Raspberry Filling ✳ 56

Gingerbread Cupcakes with Cinnamon Cream
Cheese Frosting ✳ 58

Lemon Bundt Cake with Blueberry Swirl ✳ 60

Citrus Olive Oil Cake ✳ 62

Champagne Swiss Roll with
Swiss Meringue Frosting ✳ 63

Red Velvet Cupcakes with
Cream Cheese Frosting ✳ 66

Angel Food Cake ✳ 68

Chocolate Cake Every Which Way ✳ 69

Hummingbird Cake

When Joe and I moved to Raleigh, North Carolina, we were so happy to live near an amazing food scene. One evening, we went to a well-known diner downtown. There, I tried hummingbird cake for the first time, and it had the most amazing flavors—banana, pineapple, and spices. It was sweet and salty with the perfect texture. Since that day, this has been one of my favorite cakes and I love being able to make it for life's special occasions.

Yield: One 9-inch (23-cm) two-layer cake

FOR THE BATTER:

3 eggs

1 cup (200 g) granulated sugar

½ cup (115 g) packed light brown sugar

1¼ cups (285 ml) vegetable oil

2 teaspoons (10 ml) vanilla extract

1 cup (150 g) chopped banana (about 1½ large bananas)

1 cup (244 g) crushed and drained pineapple

3 cups (444 g) 1:1 gluten-free flour

1 teaspoon (6 g) kosher salt (Morton's)

1 teaspoon (4.6 g) baking soda

2 teaspoons (9.2 g) baking powder

1 teaspoon (2 g) ground cinnamon

⅛ teaspoon (0.3 g) nutmeg

¾ cup (90 g) sweetened coconut flakes

1½ cups (165 g) pecans, chopped, divided

FOR THE FROSTING:

1 pound (455 g) dairy-free cream cheese, room temperature

½ cup (112 g) vegetable or canola butter, room temperature

2 teaspoons (10 ml) vanilla extract

4 to 6 cups (480 to 720 g) powdered sugar

To make the batter:

1. Place an oven rack in the center position. Preheat the oven to 350°F (180°C) and spray two 9-inch (23-cm) round cake pans with nonstick baking spray.

2. Add eggs and sugars to a stand mixer with a paddle attachment. Turn the mixer to high and blend for 3 to 5 minutes until light and frothy; the sugars should be almost dissolved. The appearance should be smoother, without a gritty texture. Reduce the speed to low and add vegetable oil, vanilla, banana, and pineapple. Mix 2 minutes and scrape down the sides.

3. Pause the mixer and add flour, salt, baking soda, baking powder, cinnamon, and nutmeg. Turn mixer to low and blend until just combined, being careful not to overmix. Use a spatula to gently fold in coconut and 1 cup (110 g) of the pecans.

4. Divide the batter evenly between the 2 pans and bake for 35 to 45 minutes or until a toothpick comes out clean. Allow your cakes to cool completely in the pans, then refrigerate the cakes until completely chilled.

To make the frosting:

1. Combine cream cheese, butter, vanilla, and 4 cups (480 g) of the powdered sugar in your stand mixer. You may need 2 more cups (240 g) of powdered sugar to help the frosting hold its shape; this will depend on the cream cheese and butter you use. Start the mixer on low to incorporate sugar, then elevate to medium/high until smooth and fluffy.

2. Apply a layer of frosting to the center of your bottom cake, then stack the second cake on top. Frost the cake and top with the remaining ½ cup (55 g) chopped pecans.

Upside-Down Pineapple Cake

This cake is a must-have for any cookout or BBQ night. The light and fluffy cake texture and sweetness from the fruit is the perfect end to a meal.

Yield: 8 servings, one 9 x 13-inch (23 x 33-cm) baking dish

12 slices pineapple

12 maraschino cherries, stems removed

1⅓ cups (267 g) granulated sugar

1 cup (225 g) vegetable or canola butter, room temperature

3 eggs

1 tablespoon (15 ml) vanilla extract

½ cup (115 g) dairy-free sour cream

½ cup (120 ml) pineapple juice

2¼ cups (333 g) 1:1 gluten-free flour

1 tablespoon (13.8 g) baking powder

¼ teaspoon (1.15 g) baking soda

½ teaspoon (3 g) kosher salt (Morton's)

1. Place an oven rack in the center position. Preheat the oven to 350°F (180°C) and spray a 9 x 13-inch (23 x 33-cm) baking dish with nonstick baking spray.

2. Cover the baking dish with a layer of pineapple slices and place a maraschino cherry in the center of each.

3. In a stand mixer with a whisk and medium bowl, combine sugar and butter. Mix on high for 5 minutes or until light and fluffy. Add the eggs and vanilla to the bowl. Mix for 3 minutes or until well incorporated. Stir in sour cream and pineapple juice and mix for 3 minutes. Scrape down the sides. Gradually add the flour, baking powder, baking soda, and salt. Mix until just incorporated, being careful not to overmix.

4. Pour the batter into the prepared baking dish. Bake for 20 to 25 minutes or until a toothpick inserted into the center comes out clean.

5. Remove from the oven and allow the cake to sit in the baking dish for 5 minutes, then flip the dish over onto a flat serving tray. Let the dish sit on top for a minute to allow the cake to release, then slowly remove the baking dish to reveal this tropical, tasty cake.

Chocolate Coconut Tres Leches Cake

This is one of my favorite cakes to make. You can really have fun with the flavors and change it up for different occasions, but please make it once as written first. Anyone who has tried it can never stop at one bite! Maybe that's why it's one of the only desserts Joe doesn't willingly share with our neighbors.

Yield: 10 servings, one 9 x 13-inch (23 x 33-cm) baking dish

FOR THE BATTER:

5 eggs, separated

1⅛ cups (225 g) granulated sugar

½ teaspoon (1 g) espresso powder

2 teaspoons (10 ml) vanilla extract

½ cup (120 ml) oat or pea-protein milk

1 cup (148 g) 1:1 gluten-free flour

½ cup (40 g) cocoa powder

2½ teaspoons (11.5 g) baking powder

½ teaspoon (3 g) kosher salt (Morton's)

FOR THE TOPPING:

1 can (12 ounces or 340 g) dairy-free evaporated milk

1 can (14 ounces or 397 g) dairy-free sweetened condensed milk

1 can (12 ounces or 340 g) unsweetened light coconut milk

8 ounces (225 g) dairy-free whipped topping

1 cup (120 g) sweetened coconut flakes

Strawberries (optional)

To make the batter:

1. Place an oven rack in the center position. Preheat the oven to 350°F (180°C) and generously spray a 9 x 13-inch (23 x 33-cm) baking dish (that's at least 2½ inches [6.5 cm] deep) with nonstick baking spray.

2. In a stand mixer with a whisk and large bowl, beat the egg whites until stiff peaks form. Set aside.

3. In another large mixing bowl, combine the egg yolks, sugar, and espresso powder. Mix on high speed for 2 to 3 minutes until the mixture turns light yellow. Incorporate the vanilla and milk. Scrape down the sides. Gradually add the flour, cocoa powder, baking powder, and salt to the mixture, mixing until just incorporated. Gently fold in the egg whites until well combined.

4. Pour batter into prepared dish and bake for 30 to 35 minutes or until a toothpick inserted into the center comes out clean.

5. Allow to cool completely at room temperature. Use a toothpick to poke holes all over the surface.

To make the topping:

1. In a large mixing bowl, combine the milks. Mix well to create the tres leches mixture.

2. Pour evenly over the cooled cake, ensuring that it seeps into the holes to soak the cake thoroughly. Cover the dish and refrigerate for at least 4 hours, allowing the cake to absorb the flavors and become moist and decadent.

3. Before serving, top with whipped topping and coconut flakes. For an optional garnish, add fresh strawberries.

Orange Creamsicle Cupcakes

Yield: 20 cupcakes

Who doesn't love a good cupcake? These orange creamsicle cupcakes are a blast from the past, inspired by the flavor from one of my favorite treats as a kid: orange creamsicle push pops. My grandma used to get them for my brother and me. I swear we'd eat the whole box in a day. Turns out, it's also the perfect flavor for cupcakes.

FOR THE BATTER:

1⅓ cups (267 g) granulated sugar

¼ cup (24 g) orange zest

½ cup (112 g) vegetable or canola butter, room temperature

½ cup (120 ml) orange juice

½ cup (115 g) dairy-free sour cream

½ tablespoon (8 ml) vanilla cream flavor or vanilla extract

3 eggs

2¼ cups (333 g) 1:1 gluten-free flour

½ teaspoon (2.3 g) baking powder

¼ teaspoon (1.15 g) baking soda

½ teaspoon (3 g) kosher salt (Morton's)

FOR THE FROSTING:

4 cups (480 g) powdered sugar

2 cups (450 g) vegetable or canola butter, room temperature

½ teaspoon (2.5 ml) vanilla cream flavor or vanilla extract

1 tablespoon (15 ml) orange juice

2 tablespoons (28 ml) oat or pea-protein milk

Orange food coloring (optional)

To make the batter:

1. Place an oven rack in the center position. Preheat the oven to 350°F (180°C) and add liners to 2 cupcake tins.

2. In a stand mixer with a whisk and large bowl, combine the sugar and orange zest. Mix well and let sit for a couple of minutes to infuse the citrus flavor into the sugar. Mix in the butter for 3 minutes. Add the orange juice, sour cream, and vanilla. Mix for 3 minutes until well combined. Add the eggs, one at a time, mixing well after each egg. Scrape down the sides.

3. In a separate bowl, whisk together the flour, baking powder, baking soda, and salt. Gradually add the dry mixture to the wet ingredients, mixing until just incorporated. Do not overmix.

4. Divide the batter equally into the prepared pans, filling each liner about two-thirds full.

5. Bake for 20 to 25 minutes or until a toothpick inserted into the center of a cupcake comes out clean. Let cool completely.

To make the frosting:

1. In a mixing bowl, combine the powdered sugar, butter, vanilla, orange juice, and milk. Using an electric mixer, mix together until light and fluffy, about 5 minutes. Add orange food coloring if desired.

2. Pipe the creamy orange frosting onto the cupcakes.

VARIATION

✻ Instead of making cupcakes, you could make a cake in a 9 x 13-inch (23 x 33-cm) baking dish.

Coconut Cake with Raspberry Filling

This coconut cake is incredibly versatile, allowing you to create cupcakes, sheet cakes, or any other desired form. The filling can be customized to your liking. I've tried passion fruit curd, lemon curd, cream cheese frosting, and blackberry jam—they all go well with this coconut cake.

Yield: 8 servings, one 8-inch (20-cm) two-layer cake

FOR THE BATTER:

1 teaspoon (5 ml) coconut extract

2 teaspoons (10 ml) vanilla extract

1/2 teaspoon (2.5 ml) almond extract

3/4 cup (165 g) vegetable or canola butter, room temperature

1 3/4 cups (350 g) granulated sugar

6 egg whites

5 ounces (140 g) dairy-free unsweetened coconut yogurt

1 cup (235 ml) coconut milk

2 1/2 cups (370 g) 1:1 gluten-free flour

1 1/2 tablespoons (20.7 g) baking powder

1/2 teaspoon (2.3 g) baking soda

1 teaspoon (6 g) kosher salt (Morton's)

1 1/2 cups (180 g) sweetened coconut flakes

FOR THE FILLING:

2 cups (250 g) fresh raspberries

1 tablespoon (8 g) cornstarch

1 teaspoon (5 ml) orange juice

1/4 cup (50 g) granulated sugar

Pinch salt

1 1/2 tablespoons (25 ml) water

To make the batter:

1. Place an oven rack in the center position. Preheat the oven to 350°F (180°C) and spray two 8-inch (20-cm) round cake pans with nonstick baking spray.

2. In a stand mixer with a whisk and large bowl, combine the extracts, butter, and sugar. Mix on high speed until light and fluffy, about 3 minutes. Add the egg whites, yogurt, and coconut milk and mix for 3 to 5 minutes. Using a spatula, scrape the sides. Add the rest of the ingredients and mix until just incorporated, being careful not to overmix.

3. Split the batter between the baking pans and bake for 25 to 30 minutes or until a toothpick comes out clean. Place the cakes on cooling racks, and let cool completely.

To make the filling:

1. In a small saucepan, add all the filling ingredients and cook for 10 minutes over medium heat, gently pressing with a fork to break down the raspberries. The sauce should be thickened.

2. Transfer to an airtight container. Cool completely.

To make the frosting:

1. In a large mixing bowl, add all the frosting ingredients and mix until smooth, light, and creamy, about 5 minutes.

2. Spread the frosting around the edge of the first layer to make a barrier, then spread the raspberry filling in the center of the first layer. Add the second cake layer and frost the entire cake.

FOR THE FROSTING:

1½ cups (337 g) vegetable or canola butter, room temperature

5½ cups (660 g) powdered sugar

1 teaspoon (5 ml) coconut extract

1 teaspoon (5 ml) vanilla extract

8 ounces (225 g) dairy-free cream cheese, room temperature

⅛ cup (28 ml) oat or pea-protein milk

VARIATION

* Instead of frosting, you can top the cake with some raspberry sauce and decorate it with coconut flakes.

Gingerbread Cupcakes with Cinnamon Cream Cheese Frosting

Gingerbread has always been one of my favorite scents, evoking a feeling of warmth and inviting comfort. These cupcakes are an absolute must-have during the cooler months. Not only can they be transformed into a cake, but they also possess a delightful sponginess and lightness, all while bursting with incredible flavor.

Yield: 12 cupcakes

FOR THE BATTER:

1/2 cup (115 g) packed light brown sugar

1 tablespoon (6 g) orange zest

1/2 cup (112 g) vegetable or canola butter, room temperature

2 eggs

1 1/2 teaspoons (7.5 ml) vanilla extract

1/2 cup (120 ml) oat or pea-protein milk

1/2 cup (170 g) molasses

1 3/4 cups (259 g) 1:1 gluten-free flour

1 teaspoon (4.6 g) baking powder

1/2 teaspoon (2.3 g) baking soda

1 teaspoon (6 g) ground ginger

2 teaspoons (5 g) ground cinnamon

1/2 teaspoon (1 g) nutmeg

1/2 teaspoon (1 g) allspice

1 teaspoon (6 g) kosher salt (Morton's)

To make the batter:

1. Place an oven rack in the center position. Preheat the oven to 350°F (180°C) and add liners to a cupcake tin.

2. In a stand mixer with a whisk and large bowl, combine the brown sugar and orange zest. Mix on high for 3 minutes. Let sit for a couple of minutes. Add the butter and mix for 3 minutes until creamy. Add the eggs, one at a time, mixing well after each addition. Add the vanilla, milk, and molasses and mix on high for 3 minutes. Scrape down the sides. Add all the dry ingredients and mix until just incorporated.

3. Divide the batter evenly into the cupcake liners, filling them to the top (these cupcakes don't rise much). Bake for 20 to 23 minutes or until a toothpick inserted into the center comes out clean. Cool completely.

To make the frosting:

1. In a large mixing bowl, combine the cream cheese, butter, vanilla, cinnamon, and orange zest (if using). Mix until smooth and well combined. Gradually add the powdered sugar, about 1/4 cup (30 g) at a time, mixing well after each addition until the frosting reaches a slightly firm consistency for piping. If needed, add the heavy cream or milk to adjust the consistency of the frosting.

2. Transfer the frosting to a piping bag with desired tip and pipe onto the cooled cupcakes.

FOR THE FROSTING:

8 ounces (225 g) dairy-free cream cheese, room temperature

¼ cup (55 g) vegetable or canola butter, room temperature

1 teaspoon (5 ml) vanilla extract

2 teaspoons (5 g) ground cinnamon

1 teaspoon (2 g) orange zest (optional)

3 to 4 cups (360 to 480 g) powdered sugar

1½ tablespoons (25 ml) dairy-free heavy cream or oat or pea-protein milk

Lemon Bundt Cake with Blueberry Swirl

Bundt cakes are perfect for entertaining, and I absolutely love making them. The wide variety of Bundt cake pans available allows you to create stunning cakes with minimal decoration needed, making them both beautiful and delicious centerpieces for any occasion. One of my favorite brands is Nordic Ware. They have such pretty designs!

Yield: One 10-inch (25-cm) Bundt cake

FOR THE SYRUP:

2 cups (290 g) blueberries

½ cup (120 ml) water

½ cup (100 g) granulated sugar

FOR THE BATTER:

1 cup (225 g) vegetable or canola butter, melted

¼ cup (24 g) lemon zest

2 cups (400 g) granulated sugar

5 eggs

1 cup (230 g) dairy-free sour cream

¼ cup (60 ml) freshly squeezed lemon juice

½ teaspoon (2.5 ml) almond extract

1½ teaspoons (7.5 ml) vanilla extract

3½ cups (518 g) 1:1 gluten-free flour

1 teaspoon (6 g) kosher salt (Morton's)

4 teaspoons (18.4 g) baking powder

FOR THE GLAZE:

2 cups (240 g) powdered sugar

½ teaspoon (2.5 ml) vanilla extract

3 tablespoons (60 g) reserved blueberry syrup

To make the syrup:

1. Place an oven rack in the center position. Preheat your oven to 350°F (180°C) and spray a 10-inch (25-cm) Bundt pan with nonstick baking spray. This is key to having your cake come out smoothly when finished.

2. In a small saucepan, combine the blueberries, water, and sugar. Place over medium heat and simmer for about 10 to 15 minutes until the blueberries transform into a velvety syrup. While that's simmering, make the batter.

3. Reserve 3 tablespoons (60 g) of this syrup for the glaze.

To make the batter:

1. In a stand mixer with a whisk and large bowl, mix the melted butter, lemon zest, and sugar for about 3 minutes. Add the eggs, one at a time, ensuring they're well incorporated. Scrape down the sides. Add sour cream, lemon juice, and extracts. Scrape down the sides again.

2. In another bowl, whisk or sift together the flour, salt, and baking powder. Gradually add the dry ingredients into the wet mixture, stirring until everything is just blended and not overmixed.

3. Pour half of the batter into your prepared Bundt pan. Gently layer on the blueberry syrup, letting it gracefully swirl through the batter. Pour the remaining cake batter on top.

4. Bake for 45 to 60 minutes. You'll know it's ready when a toothpick inserted halfway comes out clean.

5. Carefully remove and let rest for 5 minutes. After this short break, flip the cake onto a wire rack and let it cool down entirely.

To make the glaze:

1. In a bowl, combine powdered sugar, vanilla, and reserved blueberry syrup. Mix until smooth.

2. Gently pour this glaze over your cooled cake.

Citrus Olive Oil Cake

I used to shy away from trying or ordering olive oil cakes, believing they would be too heavy. However, the first time I made one, I became absolutely obsessed. To my surprise, the olive oil added a richness and made the cake so moist—and not too heavy!

Yield: 8 servings, one 9-inch (23-cm) square pan or a 10-inch (25-cm) round pan

FOR THE BATTER:

1 tablespoon (6 g) orange zest

1 teaspoon (2 g) lime zest

2 teaspoons (4 g) lemon zest

1¼ cups (250 g) granulated sugar

3 eggs

¾ cup (175 ml) olive oil

¾ cup (173 g) dairy-free sour cream

2 tablespoons (28 ml) orange juice

1 teaspoon (5 ml) vanilla extract

2¼ cups (333 g) 1:1 gluten-free flour

1 tablespoon (13.8 g) baking powder

¼ teaspoon (1.5 g) kosher salt (Morton's)

FOR THE GLAZE:

2 tablespoons (28 ml) orange juice

1 tablespoon (6 g) orange zest

2 cups (240 g) powdered sugar

To make the batter:

1. Place an oven rack in the center position. Preheat the oven to 375°F (190°C). Spray a 9-inch (23-cm) cake pan or bread pan with nonstick baking spray.

2. In a stand mixer with a paddle, combine the zests and sugar. Mix well for a 2 minutes to infuse the sugar with the citrus. Add the eggs, olive oil, sour cream, orange juice, and vanilla. Scrape down the sides. Mix until well combined.

3. In a separate bowl, whisk together the flour, baking powder, and salt. Gradually add the dry ingredients to the wet mixture. Mix until just incorporated, being careful not to overmix.

4. Pour the batter into the prepared pan, spreading evenly. Bake for 45 to 60 minutes, until a toothpick inserted into the center of the cake comes out clean. Allow to cool completely before removing from the pan.

To make the glaze:

1. In a small mixing bowl, mix the ingredients together.

2. Drizzle on top of the cake.

Champagne Swiss Roll with Swiss Meringue Frosting

Elevate your celebrations with this beautiful Swiss roll. Its light and airy texture, complemented by a delightful champagne essence, makes it the ideal cake for any special occasion.

Yield: 1 Swiss roll, 8 slices

FOR THE BATTER:

4 eggs, separated, plus 2 egg whites

1 drop pink food coloring

2/3 cup (133 g) granulated sugar

1/3 cup (80 ml) champagne

1 teaspoon (5 ml) champagne flavor extract (optional, to intensify flavor)

1¼ cups (185 g) 1:1 gluten-free flour

1 teaspoon (4.6 g) baking powder

2 tablespoons (15 g) powdered sugar

FOR THE FILLING:

6 egg whites

2 cups (400 g) granulated sugar

FOR ASSEMBLY:

2 cups (290 g) fresh berries (your choice)

To make the batter:

1. Place an oven rack in the center position. Preheat your oven to 350°F (180°C). Spray a 10 x 15-inch (23 x 38-cm) baking sheet with nonstick baking spray and cover with a sheet of waxed paper.

2. In a stand mixer with a whisk and large bowl, add the 4 egg yolks and pink food coloring. Beat for about 3 minutes until well combined. Continue to beat and gradually add sugar, champagne, and extract, if using. Beat for 3 minutes until the mixture becomes creamy and well incorporated. On low, mix in flour and baking powder until just incorporated. Do not overmix.

3. In a separate large mixing bowl, use a mixer with a whisk to beat the 6 egg whites until stiff peaks form. Carefully fold the beaten egg whites into the cake batter. Use a gentle folding motion to maintain the fluffiness of the egg whites.

4. Pour the batter onto the prepared baking sheet and spread evenly. Bake for 10 to 15 minutes or until a toothpick inserted into the center comes out clean.

5. Sprinkle some powdered sugar evenly over the cake. Place a clean towel on top of the cake and carefully, starting from one end, roll the cake and waxed paper along with the towel. Place the rolled cake on a cooling rack to cool completely. This will help it maintain its shape.

✳ **continued** ✳

✳

To make the filling:

1. In a glass bowl, combine egg whites and sugar and whisk for 4 minutes until well combined.

2. Place a pot of water over medium-low heat on the stove. Set the glass bowl on top of the pot, ensuring that the water does not touch the bottom of the bowl.

3. Whisk the mixture continuously for 5 to 8 minutes until it becomes slightly foamy and the sugar granules are melted. Use a food thermometer to ensure that the temperature reaches 160°F (71°C).

4. Carefully remove the glass bowl from the double boiler and pour into a mixing bowl. Use a mixer on high speed to whip for 10 minutes. The Swiss meringue should become glossy and form stiff peaks.

To assemble:

1. Slowly unroll the cake, removing the towel and waxed paper as you go.

2. Pipe a line of filling about 1 inch (2.5 cm) from all sides of the cake. Then pipe in the rest of the area evenly, using about half of the filling.

3. Carefully roll up the cake, starting from one end.

4. Top with the remaining half of the Swiss meringue and fresh berries.

Red Velvet Cupcakes with Cream Cheese Frosting

Red velvet is one of my favorite cupcake flavors. It was one of the hardest recipes for me to nail as gluten- and dairy-free. This took dozens (but it felt like hundreds) of tries to get the perfect texture. These cupcakes are light and fluffy and super easy to make. Do let them cool completely before frosting, though.

Yield: 24 cupcakes

FOR THE BATTER:

2 eggs

2 cups (400 g) granulated sugar

2¹/₂ tablespoons (38 ml) red food coloring

2 teaspoons (10 ml) vanilla extract

1 cup (235 ml) oat or pea-protein milk

¹/₂ cup (120 ml) vegetable oil

2¹/₂ cups (370 g) 1:1 gluten-free flour

3 tablespoons (15 g) cocoa powder

1¹/₂ teaspoons (6.9 g) baking powder

1¹/₂ teaspoons (6.9 g) baking soda

1 teaspoon (6 g) kosher salt (Morton's)

1 cup (235 ml) fresh-brewed coffee

FOR THE FROSTING:

1 pound (455 g) dairy-free cream cheese

¹/₂ cup (112 g) vegetable or canola butter, room temperature

2 teaspoons (10 ml) vanilla extract

5 to 7 cups (600 to 840 g) powdered sugar

To make the batter:

1. Place an oven rack in the center position. Preheat your oven to 350°F (180°C) and generously spray 2 cupcake pans with nonstick baking spray.

2. In a stand mixer with a whisk and large bowl, beat eggs and sugar on high for 3 minutes until well combined. Add food coloring, vanilla, milk, and oil. Mix thoroughly and scrape down the sides. Gradually add flour, cocoa powder, baking powder, baking soda, and salt. Mix until just incorporated. Add coffee—this will give your cake a rich and bold flavor. Stir until well combined.

3. Divide batter evenly into the prepared cupcake pans. The cups should be about two-thirds full. Bake for about 20 to 25 minutes, or until a toothpick inserted comes out clean. Cool cupcakes completely in the pans.

To make the frosting:

1. In a large mixing bowl, combine the cream cheese, butter, and vanilla. Mix until smooth and creamy. Gradually add 5 cups (600 g) of the powdered sugar. The amount needed may vary based on the cream cheese used and your desired frosting consistency. Be cautious not to overmix, as it can become too creamy. If you prefer a firmer frosting, add more powdered sugar until you reach your desired texture.

2. Spread generously over your cupcakes and get ready to dig in!

Angel Food Cake

Angel food cake is a fun base for dessert. With its airy and light texture, it serves as a perfect canvas for exploring a wide array of toppings. From classic vanilla to exotic options like coconut or mango, you have the option to customize this cake to your liking as well.

Yield: 8 servings

12 egg whites

2 teaspoons (10 ml) vanilla extract

2 teaspoons (7 g) cream of tartar

1½ cups (180 g) powdered sugar, divided

Pinch salt

1 cup (148 g) 1:1 gluten-free flour

1. Place an oven rack in the center position. Preheat the oven to 325°F (170°C). Use a traditional angel food cake pan and do not grease the pan.

2. In a stand mixer with a whisk and large bowl, combine the egg whites, vanilla, and cream of tartar. Mix on high for a couple of minutes until stiff peaks start to form. Gradually add 1 cup (120 g) of the powdered sugar and a pinch of salt, continuing to mix until the mixture appears glossy and well incorporated. Set aside.

3. In a separate bowl, sift together flour and remaining powdered sugar. This step ensures a smoother and lighter cake texture.

4. Gently fold a couple of tablespoons of the flour mixture into the egg whites. The goal is to keep the batter light and airy, so handle it with care. Add the remaining flour mixture in about four batches, folding gently each time.

5. Carefully spoon the batter into the ungreased pan. Gently tap or move the pan around on a flat surface to even out the top of the cake. Bake for 40 to 45 minutes, or until a toothpick inserted halfway through comes out clean.

6. Remove the cake from the oven and immediately place the pan upside down on a cooling rack. This step ensures the cake retains its airy structure and doesn't collapse. Allow the cake to cool in this position for about 1 hour or until completely cooled. Gently run a knife around the edge of the cake to remove it from the pan, making sure not to damage its delicate texture.

NOTE

* When working with egg whites, make sure your mixing bowl and whisk are completely dry and clean. The egg whites should be cold.

Chocolate Cake Every Which Way

This recipe is Joe's favorite cake, which means I get plenty of practice making it! It is easy to see the appeal: it's a perfect, classic, decadent chocolate cake. Perhaps because I have made it so many times, I love creating new variations by changing the frosting. This cake can go from chocolate to German chocolate to chocolate peanut butter by just adding some simple ingredients. It's the perfect base for many different flavors!

Yield: 8 slices, one 8-inch (20-cm) two-layer round cake

FOR THE BATTER:

2 eggs

2 cups (400 g) granulated sugar

2 teaspoons (10 ml) vanilla extract

5 ounces (140 g) dairy-free sour cream

½ cup (120 ml) vegetable oil

1 teaspoon (2 g) espresso powder

1 cup (235 ml) fresh-brewed coffee

2 cups (296 g) 1:1 gluten-free flour

¾ cup (60 g) cocoa powder

1½ teaspoons (6.9 g) baking powder

1½ teaspoons (6.9 g) baking soda

1 teaspoon (6 g) kosher salt (Morton's)

FOR THE FROSTING:

1½ cups (337 g) vegetable or canola butter, room temperature

5 cups (600 g) powdered sugar

1 teaspoon (5 ml) vanilla extract

½ cup (120 ml) oat or pea-protein milk

1 teaspoon (2 g) espresso powder

1⅛ cups (90 g) unsweetened cocoa powder

To make the batter:

1. Place an oven rack in the center position. Preheat the oven to 350°F (180°C) and generously coat two 8-inch (20-cm) round cake pans with nonstick baking spray.

2. In a stand mixer with a whisk, add the eggs and sugar. On high speed, beat for 3 minutes until fluffy.

3. In a separate medium mixing bowl, combine vanilla, sour cream, oil, and espresso powder. Lightly mix. Add to stand mixer. Mix in the coffee. Blend until combined; do not overmix. Scrape down the sides.

4. In another bowl, sift the dry ingredients. Add to the mixer on low speed until incorporated. Do not overmix, or the cake will be dense.

5. Divide the batter into prepared pans. Bake for 35 to 45 minutes or until a toothpick emerges clean and the cakes bounce lightly when pressed on the top. Cool completely in the pans. Invert the cake pans onto a cooling rack, giving them a gentle shake to release from the pan.

To make the frosting:

1. In your stand mixer, combine all ingredients for the frosting. Mix on high until fully incorporated, creamy, and smooth. Frost the cake to your liking.

✳ **continued** ✳

✳

69

Variations

Want to change it up? Here are some frosting variations.

Peanut Butter Frosting

1 pound (455 g) dairy-free cream cheese

2 teaspoons (10 ml) vanilla extract

5 cups (600 g) powdered sugar

2 cups (520 g) creamy peanut butter

Combine all ingredients in a stand mixer. Mix on low until incorporated, then switch to high until smooth and creamy.

German Chocolate Frosting

3 egg yolks

1 cup (225 g) packed light brown sugar

1 cup (235 ml) dairy-free evaporated milk

½ cup (112 g) vegetable or canola butter

1 teaspoon (5 ml) vanilla extract

2 cups (220 g) chopped pecans

1 cup (120 g) sweetened coconut flakes

In a saucepan over medium heat, combine egg yolks, brown sugar, evaporated milk, and butter. Stir continuously with a silicone whisk for 8 to 10 minutes until the mixture reduces slightly and turns a caramel color. Add vanilla, stir until combined, and remove from heat. Once cool, stir in pecans and coconut. Store in an airtight container for up to 2 weeks. Bring to room temperature before using.

CHAPTER 4

Cheesecakes, Puddings, and Custards

Vanilla Crème Brûlée ✳ 75

Sticky Date Pudding ✳ 76

Rainbow Confetti Cheesecake ✳ 79

Peaches and Cream Cheesecake Bars ✳ 80

Bananas Foster Cheesecake ✳ 83

Basque Cheesecake with Strawberry Sauce ✳ 84

Black Forest Mini Cheesecake Bites ✳ 87

Flan ✳ 88

Tangy Lemon Cheesecake with
Blueberry Sauce ✳ 91

Pecan Pie Cheesecake Bars ✳ 92

Vanilla Bean Cheesecake ✳ 95

Vanilla Crème Brûlée

Crème brûlée is one of those desserts that you'd think was tough to make, but once you get the hang of it, it's one of the easiest desserts when you want to impress someone. They must be chilled before eating, but they hold up great in the fridge for up to 1 week—so you can pull one out, brûlée the sugar on top, and have a fancy treat anytime!

Yield: 4 servings

5 egg yolks, room temperature

⅓ cup (67 g) granulated sugar (I used vanilla-flavored sugar), plus 1½ teaspoons (6.5 g) per ramekin

2 cups (475 ml) dairy-free heavy cream

2 teaspoons (10 g) vanilla bean paste

1. Place an oven rack in the center position. Preheat the oven to 350°F (180°C). Prepare an 8 x 8-inch (20 x 20-cm) baking dish that is at least 2 inches (5 cm) deep, along with four 6-ounce (175 ml) ramekins that will fit inside the dish.

2. Put 1½ cups (355 ml) of water on the stovetop and bring to a boil.

3. In a mixing bowl, combine the egg yolks and ⅓ cup (67 g) of the sugar. Whip together for roughly 5 minutes until the mixture becomes light yellow.

4. In a small saucepan, add the heavy cream and vanilla bean paste. Place the pot over medium-low heat until it reaches a slow boil, with small bubbles forming around the edges—but not a full boil. Remove the pot from the heat.

5. While whisking the egg mixture, slowly pour the heated cream into the bowl. Continue whisking until well combined.

6. Pour evenly into the prepared ramekins. Create a water bath by carefully adding the boiling water to the dish. Place the ramekins into the baking dish, ensuring they are stable. Bake for 30 minutes. Let ramekins cool in the baking dish for 30 minutes.

7. Remove the ramekins and refrigerate them for at least 6 hours. Before serving, sprinkle 1½ teaspoons (6.5 g) of the sugar evenly on top of each crème brûlée. Use a small kitchen blowtorch to caramelize the sugar until it forms a golden-brown crust.

NOTE

✳ If you do not have a kitchen blowtorch, these can be broiled in the oven. Watch carefully so they do not burn.

Sticky Date Pudding

Fun fact: I have zero self-control around this dessert. This is one of those desserts that you will never realize how good it is until you make it—the photo doesn't do it justice. It's incredibly tasty, with all those comforting flavors, while not being too difficult to make. Make this sticky goodness and enjoy with the luscious vanilla sauce. And of course, serve it with vanilla ice cream!

Yield: 6 servings

FOR THE PUDDING:

1 cup (178 g) dates, pitted and chopped

1 teaspoon (4.6 g) baking soda

1 cup (235 ml) water, boiling

¼ cup (60 g) packed light brown sugar

6 tablespoons (85 g) vegetable or canola butter, room temperature

2 eggs

2 teaspoons (10 ml) vanilla extract

1⅓ cups (197 g) 1:1 gluten-free flour

¼ teaspoon (.06 g) ground cinnamon

⅛ teaspoon (1 g) cardamom

1 tablespoon (13.8 g) baking powder

FOR THE SAUCE:

4 egg yolks

1 teaspoon (5 ml) vanilla extract

3 tablespoons (39 g) granulated sugar

1¼ cups (285 ml) dairy-free heavy cream

To make the pudding:

1. Place an oven rack in the center position. Preheat your oven to 350°F (180°C) and coat a muffin tin with nonstick baking spray.

2. Combine dates with baking soda in a bowl, then pour the boiling water over them. Use a masher to create a luscious date paste.

3. In another bowl, whip the brown sugar and butter until light and fluffy, about 3 minutes. Incorporate eggs and vanilla. Add the remaining ingredients, including the date paste, and mix until just combined. During the mixing process, you may have to stop to scrape down the sides.

4. Divide the batter into the prepared muffin tin and bake for 30 to 35 minutes or until a toothpick comes out mostly clean. Once out of the oven, flip them over on a cooling rack.

To make the sauce:

1. Whisk together egg yolks, vanilla, and sugar.

2. Heat heavy cream in a medium saucepan until nearly boiling.

3. Add a tablespoon (15 ml) of hot cream to the egg mixture and stir to temper. Pour the egg mixture into the pot. Stir continuously over low heat for 5 to 8 minutes until thickened. Enjoy immediately with your sticky date pudding.

Rainbow Confetti Cheesecake

Creating this cheesecake recipe reminded me of two of my favorite things while growing up: decadent cheesecake and fun, confetti-flecked birthday treats. Turns out, they just might be even better together. I loved being able to join these awesome memories together.

Yield: 8 slices

FOR THE CRUST:

2¾ cups (234 g) crushed sugar cookies

½ cup + 2 tablespoons (140 g) vegetable or canola butter, melted

FOR THE FILLING:

1 pound (455 g) dairy-free cream cheese, room temperature

1¼ cups (250 g) granulated sugar

1 egg

2 egg yolks

12 ounces (340 g) dairy-free sour cream

3 tablespoons (45 ml) vanilla extract (opt for high-quality for a stronger flavor)

¼ cup (48 g) sprinkles

FOR THE TOPPING:

Fresh whipped dairy-free cream or vanilla frosting

Fuschia gel food coloring

Sprinkles

To make the crust:

1. To make the crust, place the sugar cookies in a blender and pulse into fine crumbs.

2. In a mixing bowl, thoroughly mix the melted butter with the cookie crumbs until they form together.

3. Spray a 9-inch (23-cm) springform pan with nonstick baking spray. Press the mixture evenly onto the sides and bottom of the springform pan using a measuring cup or mason jar.

4. Set the pan in the refrigerator to chill while you prepare the filling.

To make the filling:

1. Place an oven rack in the center position. Preheat your oven to 325°F (170°C).

2. In a stand mixer with a whisk or paddle and large bowl, beat the cream cheese on high until smooth and creamy. Add the sugar, sour cream, and vanilla. Mix until well combined. Introduce the egg and yolks to the mixing bowl, one at a time, ensuring thorough mixing. Scrape down the sides, add food coloring, and mix again. Gently fold in the sprinkles to distribute them evenly.

3. Pour the cheesecake mixture into the prepared springform pan. Place the pan on a baking sheet and bake for 55 to 65 minutes until set, with a slightly jiggly center. Be careful not to overbake—the jiggle is good and needed to ensure the proper texture. Cool at room temperature for 1 hour. Transfer to the fridge and chill for at least 6 hours before serving.

To make the topping:

1. Add a generous layer of whipped cream or pipe vanilla frosting on top, then add sprinkles.

Peaches and Cream Cheesecake Bars

This delightful dessert embodies the essence of summertime bliss, combining the lusciousness of ripe peaches with the creamy goodness of cheesecake.

Yield: 24 bars, one 9-inch (23-cm) square baking dish

FOR THE CRUST:

11 ounces (312 g) gluten-free vanilla wafer cookies, finely crumbled

7 tablespoons (98 g) vegetable or canola butter, melted

FOR THE FILLING:

1 pound (455 g) dairy-free cream cheese, room temperature

1¼ cups (150 g) powdered sugar

2 teaspoons (10 ml) vanilla cream-flavored extract or vanilla extract

2 eggs

2 cups (340 g) diced peaches

FOR THE TOPPING:

1 package (3 ounces or 85 g) peach-flavored gelatin

2 cups (340 g) fresh or (500 g) frozen peaches

Dairy-free whipped cream (optional)

Fresh peach slices (optional)

To make the crust:

1. Place an oven rack in the center position. Preheat the oven to 350°F (180°C). Line a 9-inch (23-cm) square baking dish with parchment paper.

2. In a mixing bowl, combine the crumbs and melted butter, ensuring every crumb is coated in buttery goodness.

3. Press the mixture firmly into the bottom of the prepared baking dish. Bake for 10 minutes, allowing it to set and lightly brown.

To make the filling:

1. In a stand mixture with a whisk or paddle and large bowl, whip the cream cheese until smooth. Mix in the powdered sugar, extract, and eggs on high until smooth and creamy. Scrape down the sides and mix again. Gently fold in the peaches, ensuring they are evenly distributed.

2. Pour over the prebaked crust, spreading it evenly.

To make the topping:

1. In a mixing bowl, prepare the peach-flavored gelatin according to the package instructions, ensuring it is properly dissolved. Add the fresh or frozen peaches into the gelatin mixture.

2. Spoon the gelatin over the cream cheese layer, covering it completely. Place the baking dish in the refrigerator and let chill for at least 4 hours, allowing the layers to set and the flavors to meld together.

NOTE

✳ Before serving, you can top the chilled bars with whipped cream and fresh peach slices for an extra touch of elegance and flavor.

Bananas Foster Cheesecake

If the Peaches and Cream Cheesecake Bars on page 80 are for summer, then this Bananas Foster Cheesecake is for fall. Well, it's one of my favorite cheesecakes to make any time of year, if I'm being honest. It's a wonderful combination of bananas, cinnamon, brown sugar, walnuts, and rum that makes the most flavor-packed cheesecake!

Yield: 8 servings, one 8-inch (20-cm) pan

FOR THE CRUST:

½ cup (112 g) vegetable or canola butter, melted

2½ cups (300 g) gluten-free graham cracker crumbs

½ cup (60 g) walnuts, finely minced

FOR THE FILLING:

6 ounces (170 g) dairy-free cream cheese, room temperature

12 ounces (340 g) dairy-free sour cream

1 egg

2 egg yolks

1 cup (200 g) granulated sugar

¼ cup (60 g) packed light brown sugar

2 tablespoons (28 ml) vanilla extract

1 cup (225 g) mashed banana (about 2 large bananas)

FOR THE SAUCE:

2 tablespoons (28 g) vegetable or canola butter

1 teaspoon (5 ml) vanilla extract

¼ cup (60 g) packed light brown sugar

Pinch salt

¼ teaspoon (0.6 g) ground cinnamon

¼ cup (60 ml) spiced rum

½ cup (60 g) walnuts

1 banana, sliced

To make the crust:

1. To start, mix melted butter, graham cracker crumbs, and crumb-texture walnuts in a medium bowl.

2. Press evenly into an 8-inch (20-cm) springform pan using a measuring cup or mason jar. Chill in the fridge.

To make the filling:

1. Place an oven rack in the center position. Preheat your oven to 325°F (170°C).

2. In a stand mixer with a whisk or paddle and large bowl, blend cream cheese until smooth. Add sour cream, then egg and yolks, one at a time, mixing until silky smooth. Mix in sugars, vanilla, and banana, mixing on high until fully incorporated. Scrape down the sides and mix again.

3. Pour the filling into the pan, spreading evenly. Place the springform pan on a baking sheet. Bake for 50 to 60 minutes without opening the oven to maintain the perfect cheesecake consistency. Let set at room temperature for 1 hour, then place in the fridge for 6 hours minimum. Run a knife along the edges of the crust/pan side to release the crust. Remove the sides of the pan.

To make the sauce:

1. In a large skillet over medium heat, combine butter, vanilla, brown sugar, salt, cinnamon, and rum. Stir until the sugar melts, about 10 minutes, then add walnuts and banana. Cook until thick enough to coat the back of a spoon, 5 to 8 minutes.

2. Cool for 3 minutes before generously pouring over the entire cheesecake or individual slices. If you opt for the latter, store in an airtight container and warm before serving.

*

Basque Cheesecake with Strawberry Sauce

The moment my eyes landed on my Instagram friend Albana's luscious Basque cheesecake, I knew I needed it in my life! Note that this style stands apart from the traditional cheesecake. It doesn't have a crust and is almost like a custard/cheesecake mix. The "burnt" character is key too.

Yield: 6 to 8 slices, one 9-inch (23-cm) square or a 10-inch (25-cm) round pan

FOR THE CHEESECAKE:

2 tablespoons (28 g) vegetable or canola butter

1 tablespoon (6 g) orange zest

1½ pounds (680 g) dairy-free cream cheese, room temperature

1⅓ cups (267 g) granulated sugar

2 cans (14 ounces or 395 g each) coconut cream, unshaken (see note)

6 eggs

¾ teaspoon (4.5 g) kosher salt (Morton's)

2 teaspoons (10 g) vanilla bean paste

½ cup (74 g) 1:1 gluten-free flour

FOR THE SAUCE:

2 cups (290 g) strawberries, sliced

1 orange, juiced and zested

2 tablespoons (26 g) granulated sugar

½ teaspoon (1 g) lemon zest

1 teaspoon (5 ml) Grand Marnier

To make the cheesecake:

1. Place an oven rack in the center position. Preheat your oven to 400°F (200°C). This recipe works well with either a 9-inch (23-cm) square or a 10-inch (25-cm) round springform pan.

2. Begin by buttering the pan, ensuring it is coated. Then, line the pan twice with parchment paper, leaving some overhang for easy removal.

3. In a stand mixer with a whisk or paddle and medium bowl, combine the orange zest and cream cheese. Beat the mixture on high until smooth. Incorporate sugar. Mix on high speed for 3 minutes. Next, add the hardened coconut cream (see note), eggs, salt, and vanilla bean paste. Mix on high until smooth. Scrape down the sides and mix again. Gradually add flour, mixing until just incorporated. Do not overmix.

4. Pour the batter into the prepared pan and place on a baking sheet. Bake for 60 to 70 minutes, or until the center of the cheesecake jiggles slightly and the edges are slightly golden brown. Cool to room temperature in the pan. Finally, transfer to the refrigerator to chill for at least 4 hours.

To make the sauce:

1. Add all the ingredients to a medium saucepan and place over medium-low heat. Cook for 20 minutes or until the strawberries break down and the sauce thickens. Remove from heat and let cool completely. Generously pour over the entire cheesecake or individual slices. If you opt for the latter, store in an airtight container.

NOTE

✳ We will use only the hardened white part of the coconut cream, so be sure not to shake or disturb the cans too much. That way, the liquid and solid will separate, and it will be easy to pour off the liquid and then add the hardened part to the recipe.

Black Forest Mini Cheesecake Bites

For years, on my birthday, my mom would make me a Black Forest cake. Over time, I eventually moved toward rich cheesecakes, yet to this day, I still love the combo of cherries and chocolate. Well, all that percolated in my head, and one day out came these mini bites. They are great for entertaining!

Yield: 20 servings

20 gluten-free chocolate sandwich cookies

1 pound (455 g) dairy-free cream cheese, room temperature

1¼ cups (250 g) granulated sugar

1½ tablespoons (25 ml) vanilla extract

1 egg

2 egg yolks

1 cup (255 g) cherry pie filling

1. Place an oven rack in the center position. Preheat the oven to 325°F (170°C). Add liners to a regular cupcake tin, then place one cookie in each liner.

2. In a stand mixer with a whisk or paddle and medium bowl, add the cream cheese and mix for a few minutes until creamy. Mix in the sugar, vanilla, and eggs for 3 minutes until smooth. Scrape down the sides and mix again.

3. Use a spoon to add about 3 tablespoons of the mixture to the cupcake liners. Bake your mini cheesecakes at 350°F (180°C) for 20 to 25 minutes or until set. It will have a slight jiggle when shaken. Cool for 1 hour at room temperature. Refrigerate for 2 hours.

4. When ready to eat, top your mini cheesecakes with 1 tablespoon (16 g) of cherry pie filling.

Flan

Flan is a dessert that's a breeze to prepare, except for the caramel creation. The secret to perfecting caramel lies in patience: keep it on low heat, take your time, and resist the urge to stir excessively.

Yield: 6 servings

1½ cups (300 g) granulated sugar, divided

4 eggs

1 egg yolk

1 tablespoon (15 ml) vanilla extract

2¼ cups (535 ml) oat or pea-protein milk

1. Place an oven rack in the center position. Preheat your oven to 300°F (150°C). Place six 6-ounce (175 ml) ramekins in a baking dish that's at least 2 inches (5 cm) deep. Fill the dish with boiling water to create a water bath.

2. In a medium mixing bowl, combine ¼ cup (50 g) of the sugar, eggs, yolk, vanilla, and milk. Mix until well combined and set this aside.

3. In a small saucepan, add the remaining 1¼ cups (250 g) of sugar. Place the pot over low to medium-low heat. It will take about 10 minutes for the sugar to turn into caramel. Keep an eye on it. Once you notice the sugar starting to turn a golden color, gently stir it with a wooden spoon. Allow the caramel to reach a light to medium golden-brown color, then remove it from the heat.

4. Spoon the caramel evenly into the bottom of each ramekin and pour the milk and egg mixture into the ramekins. Bake for 45 to 60 minutes. You'll know it's done when the flan no longer jiggles. Remove the ramekins from the water bath. Cool at room temperature for 1 hour, and then refrigerate for at least 6 hours before serving.

5. When ready to serve, run a knife along the edge of each ramekin to loosen the flan. Place a plate on top of the ramekin and flip it upside down to release the flan.

Tangy Lemon Cheesecake with Blueberry Sauce

When I create recipes, I don't want them to just be the best gluten- and dairy-free dish someone has had; I want everyone, regardless of their diet, to fall in love with it. This dairy-free lemon cheesecake with blueberry sauce was one of the first dishes that inspired me on this path.

Yield: 8 servings, one 9-inch (23-cm) pan

FOR THE CRUST:

2¾ cups (330 g) gluten-free graham cracker crumbs

½ cup + 2 tablespoons (140 g) vegetable or canola butter, melted

½ teaspoon (1 g) ground cinnamon

FOR THE FILLING:

1 pound (455 g) dairy-free cream cheese, room temperature

1¼ cups (250 g) granulated sugar

2 tablespoons (12 g) lemon zest

2 tablespoons (28 ml) lemon juice

12 ounces (340 g) dairy-free sour cream

1 tablespoon (15 ml) vanilla extract (use high quality for deeper flavor)

1 egg

2 egg yolks

FOR THE SAUCE:

12 ounces (340 g) fresh or frozen blueberries

½ cup (100 g) granulated sugar

½ cup (120 ml) water

To make the crust:

1. Add the graham cracker crumbs, butter, and cinnamon to a medium bowl and combine.

2. Spray a 9-inch (23-cm) springform pan with nonstick baking spray. Press in the crust mixture to create an even layer on the bottom and up onto the sides. The bottom of a measuring cup or a mason jar can be used for this. Refrigerate the crust.

To make the filling:

1. Preheat the oven to 325°F (170°C).

2. In a stand mixer with a whisk or paddle and bowl, mix cream cheese until creamy and smooth. Mix in the sugar, lemon zest, lemon juice, sour cream, and vanilla. Mix in the eggs and yolks, one at a time, until incorporated. Scrape down the sides and mix again.

3. Pour over the prepared crust. Place the springform pan on a baking sheet and bake for 55 to 60 minutes. The center should jiggle and not be shiny. It's crucial not to open the oven door during this time to ensure the perfect texture.

4. Cool at room temperature for 1 hour. Refrigerate for at least 6 hours. Run a knife along the edges of the crust/springform pan side to release the crust and remove the sides of the pan.

To make the sauce:

1. In a small saucepan, combine the blueberries, sugar, and water. Place over medium heat and stir gently to dissolve the sugar. Simmer for about 25 minutes, stirring occasionally. The blueberries will release their juices and the sauce will start to thicken. Continue simmering until the sauce reaches your desired consistency. Remember that it will thicken further as it cools.

2. Transfer the sauce to an airtight container to cool. Pour over the entire cheesecake or one slice at a time.

Pecan Pie Cheesecake Bars

This is the perfect blend of two of my absolute favorite desserts, all in a convenient and handheld form. While not as intuitive as some of my other cheesecakes, trust me: these just work. They are a must-have for Thanksgiving!

Yield: 24 servings, one 9 x 13-inch (23 x 33-cm) baking dish

FOR THE CRUST:

4 cups (480 g) gluten-free ginger snap cookie or graham cracker crumbs

2 tablespoons (26 g) granulated sugar

¾ cup (165 g) vegetable or canola butter, melted

FOR THE FILLING:

1 pound (455 g) dairy-free cream cheese, room temperature

8 ounces (225 g) dairy-free sour cream

1 egg

2 egg yolks

2 tablespoons (28 ml) vanilla extract

½ cup (115 g) packed light brown sugar

½ cup (100 g) granulated sugar

1 teaspoon (2 g) ground cinnamon

FOR THE TOPPING:

1 cup (225 g) packed light brown sugar

⅓ cup (109 g) light corn syrup

⅔ cup (160 ml) dairy-free heavy whipping cream

¼ cup (55 g) vegetable or canola butter

½ teaspoon (3 g) kosher salt (Morton's)

2 teaspoons (10 ml) vanilla extract

2½ cups (275 g) chopped pecans

To make the crust:

1. Place an oven rack in the center position. Preheat the oven to 350°F (180°C).

2. Combine crumbs with sugar and butter in a bowl. Mix until fully incorporated.

3. Press the crust mixture firmly onto the bottom of a 9 x 13-inch (23 x 33-cm) baking dish (at least 2 inches [5 cm] deep), ensuring an even layer. Using the bottom of a mason jar or measuring cup is helpful for this. Refrigerate.

To make the filling:

1. In a stand mixer with a whisk or paddle and large bowl, blend the cream cheese until smooth and creamy. Add sour cream, egg, yolks, and vanilla, continuing to mix until thoroughly combined and smooth. Incorporate sugars and cinnamon. Scrape down the sides and mix again.

2. Pour the mixture onto the prepared crust, spreading it evenly.

To make the topping:

1. In a saucepan, combine the sugar, corn syrup, cream, butter, salt, and vanilla. Place the pot over medium-low heat and cook for about 5 minutes until it reaches a low boil.

2. Remove it from the heat and carefully spoon it over the cream cheese filling. Top with pecans.

3. Bake for 40 to 45 minutes until the center is barely jiggly. Cool at room temperature for 1 hour. Refrigerate for at least 6 hours. Once ready, slice to the desired size.

Vanilla Bean Cheesecake

Indulge in the ultimate versatile and heavenly cheesecake. The possibilities are endless, as this recipe can be transformed in numerous delectable ways. Elevate it by topping with luscious cherries, velvety strawberry sauce, tantalizing caramel, or decadent hot fudge, unlocking a world of exquisite flavors.

Yield: 8 servings, one 9-inch (23-cm) pan

FOR THE CRUST:

2¾ cups (330 g) gluten-free graham crackers

½ cup + 2 tablespoons (140 g) vegetable or canola butter, melted

½ teaspoon (1 g) ground cinnamon

FOR THE FILLING:

1½ pounds (680 g) dairy-free cream cheese, room temperature

12 ounces (340 g) dairy-free sour cream

1⅔ cups (333 g) granulated sugar

1½ tablespoons (23 g) vanilla bean paste

2 tablespoons (28 ml) vanilla extract (ues high quality for stronger flavor)

2 eggs

2 egg yolks

NOTE

There are so many delicious options to top this cheesecake. Here are just a few!

* Cherry pie topping
* Chocolate sauce
* Caramel sauce
* Fresh fruits, chopped
* Dairy-free whipped cream
* Blueberry sauce, see page 91
* Raspberry sauce, see page 56

To make the crust:

1. Pulse graham crackers in a blender until finely crumbled.

2. Transfer crumbs to a bowl with the melted butter and cinnamon. Thoroughly combine.

3. Spray a 9-inch (23-cm) springform pan with nonstick baking spray. Firmly press the crust onto the pan's sides and bottom with a mason jar or measuring cup, ensuring an even layer. Refrigerate.

To make the filling:

1. Place an oven rack in the center position. Preheat the oven to 325°F (170°C).

2. In a stand mixer with a whisk or paddle and large bowl, add cream cheese and mix until smooth. Mix in sour cream, sugar, vanilla bean paste, vanilla, eggs, and yolks until incorporated, roughly 2 to 4 minutes. Scrape down the sides and mix again.

3. Pour into the prepared pan and place on a baking sheet. Bake for 60 to 70 minutes. The center of the cheesecake should exhibit a gentle jiggle, while the top remains free of shine. Cool at room temperature for 1 hour. Refrigerate for a minimum of 12 hours or, ideally, overnight.

4. Run a knife along the edges of the crust/springform pan side to release the crust. Remove the sides of the pan. Slice the cheesecake and add your toppings of choice.

Chapter 5

Pies, Tarts, and Pastries

Strawberry Rhubarb Pie ✳ 98

Peach Cobbler ✳ 100

Cream Puffs with Butterscotch Pastry Cream ✳ 103

Éclairs ✳ 104

Raspberry Pistachio Galette ✳ 106

Key Lime Pie ✳ 109

French Fruit Tart ✳ 110

Dutch Apple Pie ✳ 113

Pear Frangipane ✳ 114

Strawberry Rhubarb Pie

On this page, you'll find my all-time favorite pie! My grandma used to have a large garden and always had tons of rhubarb. Every spring she would make strawberry rhubarb pies topped with vanilla ice cream. This recipe is inspired by her, but designed to be dairy- and gluten-free.

Yield: 8 servings, one 9-inch (23-cm) deep-dish pie

FOR THE CRUST:

3 cups (444 g) 1:1 gluten-free flour, plus more as needed

1 teaspoon (4.6 g) baking powder

¾ teaspoon (4.5 g) kosher salt (Morton's)

1 cup (225 g) vegetable or canola butter, cold and cubed

¾ cup (173 g) dairy-free sour cream

6 tablespoons (90 ml) sparkling water

FOR THE FILLING:

4 cups (560 g) thinly sliced rhubarb

4 cups (680 g) sliced strawberries

1 tablespoon (15 ml) orange juice

⅓ cup (43 g) cornstarch

1¼ cup (248 g) granulated sugar

Pinch salt

FOR ASSEMBLY:

1 egg

2 tablespoons (28 ml) water

2 teaspoons (9 g) granulated sugar for sprinkling

To make the crust:

1. Add flour, baking powder, and salt to a large bowl and mix thoroughly. Add the cold, cubed butter and sour cream. Work the dough quickly using your hands or a pastry cutter. The goal is to create pea-size pockets of butter within the dough, ensuring a flaky crust. Pour in the sparkling water and continue working the dough until fully incorporated. Place the dough in plastic wrap and refrigerate for 2 hours to allow it to rest and firm up.

2. Place an oven rack in the center position. Preheat the oven to 400°F (200°C).

3. Slice the dough in half and lightly flour the work surface. Work the dough gently, making it more pliable. Use flour sparingly to avoid drying out the dough. Roll out one portion of the dough to a 12-inch (30-cm) diameter and carefully transfer it to the pie dish, creating the bottom crust.

To make the filling:

1. In a large mixing bowl, mix the rhubarb, strawberries, orange juice, cornstarch, sugar, and salt until well combined. Add the filling to a 9-inch (23-cm) deep-dish pie dish.

2. Roll out the second portion of the dough in the same way to create the top crust. Place it atop the pie, trim the edges, and crimp them to seal the pie.

To assemble:

1. Whisk together the egg and water to make an egg wash. Brush the top crust with it and sprinkle sugar on top.

2. Slice 8 slits into the top of the crust to vent the steam. Place the pie dish on a baking sheet and bake at 400°F (200°C) for 20 minutes.

3. Then, reduce the temperature to 350°F (180°C) and continue baking for an additional 40 to 45 minutes or until the crust turns golden brown. Cool at room temperature for about 1 hour before serving.

Peach Cobbler

Peach cobbler, a true classic, never goes out of style. It's incredibly easy to whip up, and while you can get by with frozen, nothing beats making this with fresh, in-season peaches. You can also change out the fruit for your favorite and use the same topping. It works equally well with berries.

Yield: 8 servings, one 9 x 13-inch (23 x 33-cm) baking dish

FOR THE FILLING:

6 cups (1020 g) sliced ripe peaches

¼ cup (60 g) packed light brown sugar

¼ cup (50 g) granulated sugar

FOR THE BATTER:

½ teaspoon (3 g) kosher salt (Morton's)

½ teaspoon (1 g) ground cinnamon

¼ teaspoon (0.6 g) nutmeg

1 tablespoon (13.8 g) baking powder

1½ cups (222 g) 1:1 gluten-free flour

6 tablespoons (85 g) vegetable or canola butter

¾ cup (175 ml) dairy-free buttermilk

1 teaspoon (5 ml) almond extract

½ teaspoon (2 g) raw sugar

To make the filling:

1. Place an oven rack in the center position. Preheat the oven to 375°F (190°C). Coat a 9 x 13-inch (23 x 33-cm) baking dish with nonstick baking spray.

2. In a mixing bowl, add the peaches and sugars. Gently mix and pour into the baking dish.

To make the batter:

1. In a small mixing bowl, whisk together the milk and vinegar. Let sit for about 10 minutes to make buttermilk.

2. In a medium mixing bowl, add the dry ingredients and mix until combined. Then, add the butter and cut with a fork or a pastry cutter until pea-size crumbs are formed. Add the buttermilk and almond extract to the batter and mix until just combined.

3. Scoop dollops of the batter all over the peaches and sprinkle the raw sugar over the batter.

4. Bake for 35 to 40 minutes. Feel free to eat as-is or crown with dairy-free vanilla ice cream.

Cream Puffs with Butterscotch Pastry Cream

My mom was an amazing cook and baker. Whenever she catered a party, she would make cream puffs in the shape of a swan. The only part we were allowed to have as kids were the insides she removed from the pastry, and the leftover pastry cream in the pot. To this day, that is still my favorite part of making this recipe, although I'll eat a whole cream puff too! (Joe loves filling a cream puff with ice cream and topping it with hot fudge . . . so if that sounds good, give that a try.)

Yield: 12 cream puffs

FOR THE BATTER:

½ cup (112 g) vegetable or canola butter

1 cup (235 ml) water

1 cup (148 g) 1:1 gluten-free flour

½ teaspoon (3 g) kosher salt (Morton's)

1 teaspoon (4.6 g) baking powder

4 eggs, room temperature

FOR THE FILLING:

2 cups (475 ml) dairy-free heavy cream

1½ teaspoons (7.5 ml) vanilla extract

4 egg yolks

¾ cup (170 g) packed light brown sugar

Pinch salt

4 tablespoons (32 g) cornstarch

Powdered sugar for dusting

To make the batter:

1. Place an oven rack in the center position. Preheat the oven to 425°F (220°C) and line a cookie sheet with parchment paper.

2. Place a medium saucepan over medium heat on the stove. Add the butter and water and bring to a rapid boil. Stir in flour, salt, and baking powder with a wooden spoon until it becomes a dough ball.

3. Remove from the saucepan and place in a mixing bowl. Add one egg at a time, mixing at high speed to avoid scrambling the egg.

4. Add to a pastry bag with a large, round opening. Pipe 2-inch (5-cm) diameter cream puffs onto the parchment paper.

5. Bake for 30 to 35 minutes or until darker than golden brown. Remove from the oven and place on a wire rack. Cool completely.

6. Cut the tops off and pull out the insides, leaving the shells only.

To make the filling:

1. In a medium saucepan, combine heavy cream and vanilla, then heat over medium heat until boiling.

2. In a separate bowl, blend the yolks, brown sugar, salt, and cornstarch. Once the cream boils, reduce heat, and temper the eggs by gradually whisking in spoonfuls of cream.

3. Once tempered, combine the egg mixture with the milk in the pot and whisk until thick. Remove from the stove and transfer the pastry cream to a bowl. Completely chill the pastry cream in the fridge, covered.

4. Cut some of the top off a pastry bag and put the cooled pastry cream in. Pipe cream into the puffs, 2 inches in diameter and about 1½ inches high, and put the tops back on. Dust with powdered sugar.

*

Éclairs

The first time I ever shot live was for Amoretti, a baking products brand in California. They invited me out to create a couple of recipes in their kitchen on film. I was beyond excited! So excited, in fact, I only slept maybe two hours the night before. As soon as I showed up, they greeted my husband and I like we had been long-time friends. They made us feel so welcome and right at home. With my nerves at ease, I made these éclairs with a twist.

Yield: 6 éclairs

FOR THE BATTER:

1 cup (148 g) 1:1 gluten-free flour

½ teaspoon (3 g) kosher salt (Morton's)

1 teaspoon (3 g) arrowroot powder

½ cup (112 g) vegetable or canola butter

1 cup (235 ml) water

4 eggs, room temperature

FOR THE FILLING:

2 cups (475 ml) oat or pea-protein milk

1 teaspoon (5 g) vanilla bean paste or a whole bean

1 egg

3 egg yolks

1 cup (200 g) granulated sugar

Pinch salt

4 tablespoons (32 g) cornstarch

FOR ASSEMBLY:

1 cup (175 g) dairy-free dark chocolate

1 teaspoon (5 ml) tiramisu flavor extract (optional)

To make the batter:

1. Place an oven rack in the center position. Preheat the oven to 425°F (220°C) and line a cookie sheet with parchment paper.

2. In a bowl, mix the flour, salt, and arrowroot powder.

3. Place a pot over medium heat, add the butter and water, and bring to a rapid boil. Stir in flour mixture with a wooden spoon until it becomes a dough ball.

4. Place dough in a mixing bowl. Mix on medium speed, and add one egg at a time until incorporated.

5. Add to a pastry bag with a large, round opening. Pipe 5-inch (13-cm)–long sections on the parchment paper. Bake for 15 minutes, then reduce heat to 350°F (180°C) (don't open the oven) and bake for an additional 25 minutes.

6. Remove the tray and make a little slit on top of each shell. Place back in the oven for 5 minutes. Place on cooling racks to cool completely.

7. Slice each éclair in half and scoop out the inside.

To make the filling:

1. To a medium saucepan, add the milk and vanilla, then place over medium heat and bring to a boil. Reduce heat to low.

2. In a separate bowl, mix the egg, yolks, sugar, salt, and cornstarch. Whisk one spoonful of the milk into the egg mixture. Whisk quickly to temper the eggs. Add another spoonful and continue to whisk. Once incorporated, add the egg mixture to the pot. Continue to whisk for 3 to 5 minutes or until thickened. Remove from heat, transfer to a bowl, cover, and place in the refrigerator to chill completely.

To assemble:

1. To make the chocolate topping, add the chocolate to a microwave-safe bowl. Microwave in 30-second increments, mixing between heating sessions. Once melted, mix in the tiramisu extract, if using.

2. Dip the top of the éclair in the chocolate and fill the inside with pastry cream.

3. Place the tops on the bottoms.

Raspberry Pistachio Galette

Galettes are one of my favorite go-to desserts. They are so simple to make, yet look so elegant! You can also customize them with what you have available. For example, you could swap the pistachio butter with a chocolate hazelnut spread and add strawberries, or whatever fruit you love.

Yield: 8 servings, one 10-inch (25-cm) galette

FOR THE CRUST:

1½ cups (222 g) 1:1 gluten-free flour, plus more as needed

½ teaspoon (2.3 g) baking powder

⅜ teaspoon (2.25 g) kosher salt (Morton's)

½ cup (112 g) vegetable or canola butter, cold and cubed

⅜ cup (86 g) dairy-free sour cream

3 tablespoons (45 ml) sparkling water

FOR THE FILLING:

½ cup (130 g) pistachio butter

2 cups (250 g) fresh raspberries

FOR ASSEMBLY:

1 egg

2 tablespoons (28 ml) water

2 teaspoons (10 g) vanilla or granulated sugar

1 tablespoon (8 g) powdered sugar

¼ cup (31 g) pistachios, chopped

To make the crust:

1. Begin by combing the dry ingredients in a large mixing bowl. Add the cubed cold butter and sour cream. Work the dough swiftly, either with your hands or a pastry cutter, being mindful not to overwork it. Aim for pockets of butter, about the size of peas, to ensure flakiness. Add the sparkling water to the dough and, using your hands, work until fully incorporated.

2. Wrap the dough in plastic wrap and refrigerate for 2 hours.

3. Place an oven rack in the center position. Preheat the oven to 400°F (200°C). Line a cookie sheet with parchment paper.

4. Lightly flour your work surface.

5. Roll out the pie crust into a roughly 12-inch (30-cm) diameter circle. Place on the baking sheet.

To make the filling:

1. Spread the pistachio butter over the pie crust, leaving a 2-inch (5-cm) border. Arrange the fresh raspberries on top.

2. Gently fold the edges over (I use my bench scraper to slide underneath and then fold the edges inward).

To assemble:

1. Whisk the egg and water together to make an egg wash. Brush the sides of the crush with the egg wash, and sprinkle sugar around the edges.

2. Bake for 45 to 55 minutes or until golden brown. Cool for 30 minutes.

3. Dust with powdered sugar and top with chopped pistachios. Joe loves to add vanilla or pistachio ice cream on top.

Key Lime Pie

This is a Southern favorite! Everyone has their own spin on key lime pie—it's seriously made a million different ways. This is my favorite go-to version. It's more tart than sweet, and is easy to make. Go ahead and brighten up a summer day (or any day!).

Yield: 8 servings, one 8- or 9-inch (20- or 23-cm) pan

FOR THE CRUST:

2½ cups (300 g) gluten-free graham cracker crumbs

¾ cup (165 g) vegetable or canola butter, melted

½ cup (68 g) macadamia nuts, finely chopped

FOR THE FILLING:

1¼ cups (285 ml) key lime juice

1 ounce (28 g) unflavored gelatin

6 eggs, room temperature

2 cups (400 g) granulated sugar

2 teaspoons (4 g) lime zest

¼ cup (55 g) vegetable or canola butter

FOR THE TOPPING:

Dairy-free whipped cream

Chopped macadamia nuts

To make the crust:

1. Place an oven rack in the center position. Preheat your oven to 350°F (180°C). Spray a 8 or 9-inch (20 or 23-cm) springform pan with nonstick baking spray.

2. Combine crumbs, butter, and nuts. Firmly press into the base of the pan using a measuring cup or mason jar. Bake for 10 minutes—just enough to set. Cool completely.

To make the filling:

1. Combine key lime juice and gelatin in a small bowl. Mix well and let sit for 5 minutes.

2. In a large mixing bowl, add eggs and sugar. Beat on high speed until pale yellow, which usually takes about 3 minutes.

3. In a medium saucepan, combine the egg mixture, gelatin mixture, lime zest, and butter. Place the pot over low heat and whisk constantly until the mixture thickens, which should take approximately 5 to 10 minutes. You can increase the heat a bit after a few minutes to expedite the thickening process. Once the mixture has thickened, pour it into the prepared crust.

4. Refrigerate for 24 hours.

5. Top with whipped cream and garnish with macadamia nuts.

French Fruit Tart

Pastry cream is my love language—I could eat it by the spoonful. When it comes to desserts, I love sweet and savory, so this is one of my all-time favorites. The savory crust, the creamy pastry cream, and the fresh fruit on top make for the perfect balance.

Yield: 8 servings, one 9-inch (23-cm) pan

FOR THE FILLING:

2 cups (475 ml) oat or pea-protein milk

1 teaspoon (5 g) vanilla bean paste

3 egg yolks

1 egg

1 cup (200 g) granulated sugar

Pinch salt

¼ cup (32 g) cornstarch

FOR THE CRUST:

1³/8 cups (204 g) 1:1 gluten-free flour, plus more as needed

½ cup + 1 tablespoon (126 g) vegetable or canola butter, cold

¼ teaspoon (1.5 g) kosher salt (Morton's)

¼ cup (60 ml) water, ice-cold

FOR ASSEMBLY:

2 tablespoons (40 g) raspberry jelly, divided

1 cup (170 g) strawberries, sliced

1 kiwi, sliced

½ cup (75 g) blueberries

½ cup (65 g) raspberries

½ cup (73 g) blackberries

To make the filling:

1. In a saucepan, combine the milk and vanilla bean paste. Place over medium heat and bring to a boil. Reduce the heat to low.

2. In a mixing bowl, whisk together the egg yolks, egg, sugar, salt, and cornstarch until well mixed.

3. Whisk a spoonful of the hot milk into the egg mixture to temper it. Repeat a few times. Pour the egg mixture back into the saucepan. Whisk constantly over low heat until custard-like.

4. Pour the pastry cream into the bowl, cover it, and refrigerate to cool completely.

To make the crust:

1. In a blender or food processor, combine all crust ingredients and pulse until well combined. The mixture should have a light, almost airy texture with tiny pieces of butter. Wrap in plastic wrap and freeze for 30 minutes until firm enough to roll out.

2. Place an oven rack in the center position. Preheat the oven to 400°F (200°C). Get out a 9-inch (23-cm) tart pan.

3. Lightly flour work surface, dough, and rolling pin, then roll out the dough. Line the tart pan with the crust and trim any excess. Place a sheet of parchment paper on the crust and add ceramic weights. Bake for 25 to 30 minutes until golden brown. Allow to cool completely. Remove the weights and paper.

To assemble:

1. Brush 1 tablespoon (20 g) of the raspberry jelly over the cooled crust.

2. Pipe the chilled pastry cream onto the crust. Arrange the fruit to your liking.

3. Microwave 1 tablespoon (20 g) of the raspberry jelly for 10 seconds to melt it slightly, then brush it over the fruit for a glossy finish.

NOTES

❋ The dough can be made 7 days in advance and left in the fridge until ready to use.

❋ If you don't have ceramic weights, you can poke holes in the base of the crust with a fork to prevent it from puffing up during baking.

Dutch Apple Pie

This pie is my most requested Thanksgiving dessert. Everyone wants a big slice of this pie with vanilla ice cream, no matter how much they already ate. Luckily, this can be made a few days in advance and holds up nicely in the fridge—now that's a perfect holiday recipe.

Yield: 6 to 8 slices, 9-inch (23-cm) deep-dish pie

FOR THE CRUST:

1½ cups (222 g) 1:1 gluten-free flour, plus more as needed

½ teaspoon (2.3 g) baking powder

⅜ teaspoon (2.25 g) kosher salt (Morton's)

½ cup (112 g) cold vegetable or canola butter, cubed

⅜ cup (86 g) dairy-free sour cream

3 tablespoons (45 ml) sparkling water

FOR THE FILLING:

8 cups (1200 g) peeled and sliced Granny Smith apples

1 teaspoon (2 g) ground cinnamon

1 teaspoon (2 g) lemon zest

1 lemon, juiced

¼ teaspoon (0.5 g) allspice

2 pinches nutmeg

⅔ cup (133 g) granulated sugar

2 tablespoons (28 g) vegetable or canola butter, cubed

FOR THE TOPPING:

½ cup (74 g) 1:1 gluten-free flour

½ cup (45 g) gluten-free rolled oats

¼ teaspoon (0.5 g) allspice

½ cup (115 g) packed brown sugar

½ cup (55 g) pecans, chopped

Pinch salt

6 tablespoons (85 g) vegetable or canola butter, room temperature

To make the crust:

1. In a large bowl, add the dry ingredients and mix well. Add the butter and sour cream and work in quickly with your hands or a pastry cutter. The butter should be pea-size when done. Add the sparkling water and use your hands to work the dough quickly until incorporated. Wrap in plastic wrap and place in the fridge for 2 hours or the freezer for 30 to 45 minutes until firm.

2. Lightly flour work surface, rolling pin, and crust. Roll out to approximately a 12-inch (30-cm) diameter. Add to a 9-inch (23-cm) deep-dish pie dish. Chill in the refrigerator or freezer while making your filling.

To make the filling:

1. Place an oven rack in the center position. Preheat the oven to 375°F (190°C).

2. Combine all the filling ingredients.

3. Place the pie dish on a baking sheet in case the filling overflows. Add the filling to the chilled pie shell.

To make the topping:

1. Mix all the topping ingredients together and sprinkle over the pie.

2. Bake for a total of 60 minutes, but check after 30 minutes. If the crust is starting to turn too dark, place a sheet of foil loosely on top.

3. Allow to cool for 3 hours before serving.

*

Pear Frangipane

I'm absolutely obsessed with this tart—well, let's be honest, I pretty much like all tarts! And even though the classic recipe on page 110 gets made the most in my house, there are certainly times where I find myself craving this delicious combination of pear and almond.

Yield: 8 servings, one 9-inch (23-cm) pan

FOR THE CRUST:

1³⁄₈ cups (204 g) gluten-free 1:1 flour, plus more as needed

½ cup + 1 tablespoon (126 g) vegetable or canola butter, cold

¼ teaspoon (1.5 g) kosher salt (Morton's)

¼ cup (60 ml) water, ice-cold

FOR THE FILLING:

4 ounces (115 g) almond paste

4 tablespoons (52 g) granulated sugar

¼ cup (55 g) vegetable or canola butter, room temperature

2 teaspoons (10 ml) vanilla extract

½ teaspoon (1 g) ground cinnamon

¼ teaspoon (1.15 g) baking powder

Pinch salt

2 eggs

FOR ASSEMBLY:

2 pears

⅛ cup (12 g) sliced almonds

1 tablespoon (8 g) powdered sugar

To make the crust:

1. Combine all the crust ingredients in a blender or food processor and pulse until it reaches a light and almost airy consistency. Wrap in plastic wrap and place it in the freezer for about 20 minutes until it firms up enough for rolling.

2. Place an oven rack in the center position. Preheat your oven to 400°F (200°C).

3. Lightly flour work surface, rolling pin, and dough, then roll it out. Line a 9-inch (23-cm) tart pan, trimming any excess. Use a fork to poke holes in the bottom. Bake for 25 to 30 minutes, until a beautiful golden brown. Remove from oven and cool completely.

4. Lower the oven to 350°F (180°C).

To make the filling:

1. Combine all ingredients in a blender or food processor until the mixture is smooth and creamy, roughly 3 minutes. Pour into the cooled crust.

To assemble:

1. Choose to peel the pears or leave as they are (I prefer skin on). Slice thinly and arrange over the almond paste filling as desired.

2. Sprinkle sliced almonds over the pears.

3. Bake for 35 to 40 minutes until the top is beautifully golden brown.

4. Allow to cool completely. Dust with powdered sugar to add a touch of sweetness.

CHAPTER 6

Sweet Breads, Muffins, and Rolls

Banana Bread Cinnamon Rolls with Peanut Butter Frosting ✳ 119

Sour Cream Coffee Cake ✳ 123

Apple Sticky Buns ✳ 125

Bread Pudding with Chocolate Chips ✳ 128

French Vanilla Scones ✳ 131

Pumpkin Streusel Muffins ✳ 132

Monkey Bread ✳ 135

Orange Sweet Rolls ✳ 136

Orange Cranberry Muffins ✳ 139

Baked Fruit Donuts ✳ 140

Banana Bread Cinnamon Rolls with Peanut Butter Frosting

Cinnamon rolls were the first yeasted gluten- and dairy-free bread that I mastered. It took dozens and dozens of tries, and when that perfect batch turned out, I could've cried! If you follow me on social media, you most likely have seen these. You may have even seen them if you don't follow me, as they have gone viral a few times—in my opinion, for good reason. They are more than just a fun recipe title. They are beyond delicious! The flavor combo of the frosting with the banana bread flavor of the roll is just perfect. I obviously had to add these bad boys to my first cookbook.

Yield: 9 cinnamon rolls

FOR THE DOUGH:

⅓ cup (67 g) granulated sugar, divided

2¼ teaspoons or 1 packet (9 g) dry instant yeast

1 tablespoon (20 g) honey

½ cup (120 ml) water, warm (110°F [43°C])

6 tablespoons (85 g) vegetable or canola butter

½ cup (120 ml) oat or pea-protein milk

1 cup (225 g) ripe mashed banana (about 2 large bananas)

3½ cups (420 g) gluten-free bread flour or (518 g) 1:1 gluten-free flour, plus more as needed (see note)

1 teaspoon (6 g) kosher salt (Morton's)

1½ teaspoons (3.5 g) ground cinnamon

¼ teaspoon (0.5 g) allspice

To make the dough:

1. In a small bowl, stir together 2½ tablespoons (28 g) of the sugar with the yeast, honey, and warm water. Allow to sit for 5 minutes until a ½-inch (1-cm) foamy head develops.

2. Set your stovetop to medium heat. In a small saucepan, add butter, the remaining sugar, and milk. Scald the mixture, avoiding boiling, until bubbles form on the outside. Remove from heat.

3. Add the yeast mixture to a stand mixer with a paddle and large mixing bowl. Turn the mixer to low and add the mashed banana. While the mixer runs, gradually pour the milk mixture into the bowl.

4. In another medium-size bowl, combine flour, salt, cinnamon, and allspice. Add in 1 cup (235 ml) increments to the wet mixture. After full incorporation, mix for an additional 3 minutes.

5. Lightly flour the work surface, dough, your hands, and rolling pin. Roll dough out gently to approximately 9 x 12 inches (23 x 30 cm).

To make the filling:

1. Combine brown sugar, cinnamon, and butter. Spread over the dough.

2. Roll the dough tightly from the short side and cut into 9 slices.

* continued *

119

FOR THE FILLING:

1 cup (225 g) packed brown sugar

2 teaspoons (5 g) ground cinnamon

6 tablespoons (85 g) vegetable or canola butter

1 cup (235 ml) dairy-free heavy cream (optional)

FOR THE FROSTING:

8 ounces (225 g) dairy-free cream cheese

1 teaspoon (5 ml) vanilla extract

1½ cups (180 g) powdered sugar, plus more as needed

1 cup (260 g) creamy peanut butter

3. Butter a 9 x 13-inch (23 x 33-cm) or 12-inch (30-cm) round baking dish and add the cinnamon rolls. Cover the dish with plastic wrap and a kitchen towel, letting the dough rise until 1½ times in size, roughly 1 to 3 hours.

4. Place a rack in the center of the oven. Preheat oven to 350°F (180°C).

5. Uncover rolls. If using heavy cream, pour over before baking. This will make the cinnamon rolls gooey. Bake for 30 to 35 minutes until golden brown.

To make the frosting:

1. Mix ingredients until smooth. Add more powdered sugar to adjust the consistency as desired.

2. Cool the rolls for 5 to 10 minutes before frosting to prevent excessive melting. Generously spread the frosting over the top using a spatula or butter knife.

NOTES

✳ If you're making these cinnamon rolls gluten-free, the dough cannot be made ahead of time. The dough will stiffen, and all texture is lost.

✳ Using 1:1 gluten-free flour may result in slight cracks upon baking, but the flavor profile remains the same. On the other hand, gluten-free bread flour ensures the classic, defined shape of a traditional cinnamon roll.

✳ If you're making this dough with dairy or gluten, no measurement changes are needed. The bake time will also stay the same. Your rise time will vary slightly. Follow all the same directions.

✳ Rise time will vary based on temperature, humidity, and elevation. I've had some batches rise in 30 minutes, and others take 5 hours. A dough rising pad can help with the rise time. I use this on cooler days.

✳ If it's a humid day, avoid the plastic wrap for the rise. Just place a towel on top.

✳ Prep the work area first so you can work more efficiently. The dough is very sticky and can be tricky to roll. Avoid overflouring the surface, which leads to dry dough. A bench scraper makes rolling it and moving the slices easier.

✳ If you're using a mixer, a paddle is ideal. Never use a whisk; this will break up the dough. A dough hook can be subbed, but the dough will need to be worked a little more, and I've found this can affect the texture slightly.

✳ This dough can be made without a mixer. Follow the same steps, but instead of working the dough for 3 minutes, work for approximately 5 minutes using a wooden spoon.

✳ Gently roll out the dough; avoid pressing the air out. We want it to be light and airy.

✳ The rolls are best eaten fresh. They hold up for 2 days after baking. Microwave to soften the rolls. Do not freeze.

✳ For a change, try chocolate frosting or coffee glaze.

Classic Cinnamon Rolls

The steps and ingredients here are almost the same as the banana bread version—there are just a few tweaks.

Follow the steps of the Banana Bread Cinnamon Rolls (page 119) with a few changes. Replace the bananas with 1 cup (230 g) dairy-free sour cream or dairy-free unsweetened, plain yogurt. Omit cinnamon and allspice from the flour mixture. Make the filling as described. Omit peanut butter from the frosting and adjust the amount of powdered sugar as needed to get your desired texture. Cut into 6 rolls for larger cinnamon rolls, or for standard size, cut into 9.

Sour Cream Coffee Cake

I've found there are people who love coffee cake and those who don't. I'm not sure why this is, but I am here to convert the unbelievers with this recipe, which I think is hands down the best sour cream coffee cake ever! It's oh-so-fluffy and crumbly, perfect for treating yourself any time of the day.

Yield: 9 servings, one 8 x 8-inch (20 x 20-cm) or 9-inch (23-cm) round baking dish

FOR THE BATTER:

2/3 cup (133 g) granulated sugar

1 cup (225 g) vegetable or canola butter, room temperature

2 eggs

1½ cups (345 g) dairy-free sour cream

4 teaspoons (20 ml) vanilla extract

2 cups (296 g) 1:1 gluten-free flour

4 teaspoons (18.4 g) baking powder

½ teaspoon (2.3 g) baking soda

½ teaspoon (3 g) kosher salt (Morton's)

Pinch nutmeg

FOR ASSEMBLY:

1¼ cups (138 g) chopped pecans

1½ teaspoons (3.5 g) ground cinnamon

½ cup (115 g) packed light brown sugar

To make the batter:

1. Place an oven rack in the center position. Preheat the oven to 350°F (180°C) and generously spray an 8 x 8-inch (20 x 20-cm) or 9-inch (23-cm) round (at least 2-inch [5-cm] deep) baking dish with nonstick baking spray.

2. In a large mixing bowl, mix the sugar and butter on high speed for 3 minutes until they combine into a creamy, smooth mixture. Incorporate the eggs, sour cream, and vanilla. Mix on high for 3 minutes to ensure each ingredient is blended well. Scrape down the sides.

3. Combine the dry ingredients. Add to the wet mixture. Carefully mix until just incorporated. Overmixing can lead to a tougher texture.

To assemble:

1. In a separate bowl, combine the chopped pecans, cinnamon, and brown sugar to create the topping mixture.

2. To assemble the cake, start by pouring half of the cake batter into the prepared baking dish.

3. Sprinkle half of the topping mixture generously in the center.

4. Gently layer the remaining cake batter over the top, and finish with the rest of the topping.

5. Bake for 40 to 50 minutes. Remove when a toothpick inserted into the center comes out clean. Allow the cake to cool in the dish before serving.

* continued *

*

VARIATIONS

❋ If you're in the mood for an extra touch of sweetness, prepare a simple glaze by mixing 1½ cups (180 g) powdered sugar and 1 tablespoon (15 ml) oat or pea-protein milk together until it forms a smooth and velvety glaze. Drizzle this glaze on top of the cooled coffee cake.

❋ This recipe can be modified to add a layer cream cheese filling. Mix together 8 ounces (225 g) room temperature dairy-free cream cheese, 1 teaspoon (5 ml) vanilla extract, and 1½ cups (180 g) powdered sugar. After the first layer of cake batter, add the cream cheese layer, top with half of the crumble mixture, the rest of the batter, and then top with the rest of the crumble. Baking time will be 5 to 8 minutes longer.

❋ To make a fruit coffee cake, fold in 1 cup (150 g) fresh chopped apples or (145 g) fresh blueberries into the cake batter.

Apple Sticky Buns

Who doesn't like a delicious sticky bun? These delightful pastries are perfect for brunch. As a gluten- and dairy-free option, these sticky buns are best savored when freshly prepared. Nevertheless, if stored properly, they can still be enjoyed the next day—but not much longer.

Yield: 9 sticky buns

FOR THE DOUGH:

½ cup (125 g) applesauce

¾ cup (173 g) dairy-free Greek yogurt

1 teaspoon (2 g) ground cinnamon

⅛ teaspoon (0.2 g) allspice

⅓ cup (67 g) granulated sugar, divided

2¼ teaspoons or 1 packet (9 g) dry instant yeast

1 tablespoon (20 g) honey

½ cup (120 ml) water, warm (110°F [43°C])

6 tablespoons (85 g) vegetable or canola butter

1 teaspoon (6 g) kosher salt (Morton's)

½ cup (120 ml) oat or pea-protein milk

3½ cups (518 g) 1:1 gluten-free flour

FOR THE FILLING:

½ cup (115 g) packed light brown sugar

1½ teaspoons (3.5 g) ground cinnamon

¼ cup (55 g) vegetable or canola butter

1 cup (150 g) finely diced apples

To make the dough:

1. In a medium-size mixing bowl, create a smooth mixture by combining applesauce, yogurt, cinnamon, and allspice.

2. In another mixing bowl, combine 2½ tablespoons (28 g) of the sugar, yeast, honey, and warm water; let it sit for 5 minutes until it bubbles. It should be very foamy—if it isn't, the yeast did not activate and you should start over.

3. In a saucepan over medium heat, heat the butter, remaining sugar, salt, and milk until bubbling at the edges (avoid boiling).

4. Combine the scalded milk mixture and yeast mixture with the applesauce mixture and mix for 3 minutes. Gradually add 1 cup (148 g) of flour at a time, fully incorporating before adding more.

5. Transfer the sticky dough to a floured surface, gently rolling it out to about 9 x 12 inches (23 x 30 cm).

To make the filling:

1. Make the filling by combining all the ingredients.

2. Spread this mixture on the rolled-out dough, then roll the dough tightly by the short side and cut into 9 slices.

✳ continued ✳

✳

FOR THE BASE:

½ cup (112 g) vegetable or canola butter

1 cup (225 g) packed light brown sugar

⅓ cup (115 g) honey

½ teaspoon (3 g) kosher salt (Morton's)

2 cups (220 g) chopped pecans

To make the base:

1. In a medium-size saucepan, stir butter, brown sugar, honey, and salt over medium heat until smooth. Add chopped pecans, stirring to coat.

2. Pour the pecan mixture into a 12-inch (30-cm) skillet or a 9 x 13-inch (23 x 33-cm) baking dish, ensuring an even layer. Arrange the cinnamon rolls on top, nestling them into the gooey goodness.

3. Cover with plastic wrap and a towel, creating a warm environment. Let the rolls rise until double in size, about 2 to 3 hours.

4. Place an oven rack in the center position. Preheat the oven to 350°F (180°C).

5. Bake uncovered for 30 minutes. Cover with foil and bake for an additional 10 minutes. Remove from the oven, flip onto a serving platter while still hot, and savor the deliciousness!

Bread Pudding with Chocolate Chips

Bread pudding is like the ultimate comfort food in a dessert! I love how you can prepare this in advance—it holds up to a week in the fridge. Also, don't be shy about customizing it by substituting chocolate for your preferred fruit for a delightful twist.

Yield: 8 to 10 servings, one 7 x 10-inch (18 x 25-cm) or 9 x 13-inch (23 x 33-cm) baking dish

FOR THE BREAD PUDDING:

1 teaspoon (2 g) ground cinnamon

3 eggs

2 cups (475 ml) oat or pea-protein milk

1 tablespoon (15 ml) vanilla extract

¾ cup (150 g) granulated sugar

5 cups (175 g) gluten-free bread, cubed (1- to 2-inch [2.5 to 5-cm]), plus more as needed

1 cup (175 g) dairy-free chocolate chips

FOR THE CRÈME ANGLAISE:

3 egg yolks

½ cup (100 g) granulated sugar

1 cup (235 ml) dairy-free heavy cream

2½ teaspoons (12.5 ml) vanilla extract

NOTE

⁕ Bread pudding works best with a firmer/denser gluten-free bread. If your bread crumbles easily, I would not recommend soaking the bread for the whole 30 minutes. This will make the bread pudding mushy.

To make the bread pudding:

1. In a large bowl, combine the cinnamon, eggs, milk, vanilla, and sugar. Whisk together until well mixed, 3 to 5 minutes.

2. Add the bread pieces to the egg mixture. Gently toss and mix until the bread is evenly coated. The bread ratio may vary by 1 to 2 cups, depending on the brand being used; the bread should be 90 percent wet. Allow this mixture to sit for about 30 minutes.

3. Place an oven rack in the center position. Preheat your oven to 350°F (180°C). Spray a 7 x 10-inch (18 x 25-cm) or 9 x 13-inch (23 x 33-cm) baking dish with nonstick baking spray. Pour the soaked bread mixture into the prepared baking dish. Sprinkle the chocolate chips evenly over the top and press some down into the bread mixture.

4. Bake for 40 to 50 minutes until golden brown. Rest for about 1 hour. This allows the flavors to melt together, the bread pudding to firm up some and makes for a more enjoyable dish.

To make the crème anglaise:

1. In a mixing bowl, whisk together the egg yolks and sugar until well combined. Set aside.

2. In a saucepan, combine the heavy cream and vanilla and heat over low to medium heat. When you start to see bubbles forming along the edges, reduce the heat to low.

3. To prevent scrambling the eggs, slowly ladle a spoonful of the hot cream mixture into the egg mixture. Whisk quickly to combine. Repeat with another spoonful of hot cream. Now, whisk the egg mixture into the saucepan. Continue to whisk until the sauce thickens enough to coat the back of a spoon. This should only take a few minutes.

4. As soon as the sauce reaches the desired consistency, remove it from the heat source to prevent overcooking. Drizzle over the top of the bread pudding to serve.

French Vanilla Scones

Have you ever tried flavored sugars? They add an exciting twist to your baking recipes while giving you additional flavor boosts. Vanilla happens to be one of my all-time favorite flavors, but since a lot of the flavor comes from the flavored sugar, you can try something else if you'd like (and consider switching the paste/extract to match).

Yield: 8 scones, 7-inch (18-cm) diameter

FOR THE BATTER:

3¼ cups (481 g) + 1 tablespoon (9 g) 1:1 gluten-free flour, divided

2½ tablespoons (34.5 g) baking powder

½ teaspoon (3 g) kosher salt (Morton's)

¾ cup (165 g) vegetable or canola butter, cold and cubed

2 eggs

1½ teaspoons (7.5 ml) vanilla extract

3 tablespoons (39 g) French vanilla-flavored sugar or regular granulated sugar

FOR ASSEMBLY:

1 egg

2 tablespoons (28 ml) water

1 teaspoon (4 g) granulated sugar

To make the batter:

1. Place an oven rack in the center position. Preheat oven to 425°F (220°C). Line a cookie sheet with parchment paper, generously dusting it with 1 tablespoon (9 g) of the flour to ensure the scones release effortlessly.

2. In a mixing bowl, add the remaining flour, baking powder, and salt. Add butter, and with the pastry blender, blend until the mixture achieves a fine crumb texture, about the size of a pea.

3. In another mixing bowl, whisk together eggs, vanilla, and sugar until completely incorporated.

4. Add the dry mixture to the wet mixture. A gentle blend is key; overmixing may render the scones hard. The dough will be slightly sticky and light. This is where the magic lies for a perfect scone.

5. Carefully transfer the dough to the parchment paper. Lightly flour your hands and shape the dough into a 7-inch (18-cm) diameter, 2-inch (5-cm)-high, round scone. Slice into 8 equal wedges, like a pie.

To assemble:

1. In a small bowl, whisk the egg and water.

2. Brush the egg mixture onto the scones. Sprinkle with sugar.

3. Slide the cookie sheet into the preheated oven, letting the scones bake for 17 to 22 minutes. What's the indicator of perfection? It's a golden-brown crown and a toothpick that emerges clean from the center. Remove from oven and cool before indulging.

✳

Pumpkin Streusel Muffins

These muffins were born out of my sheer frustration while attempting to make pumpkin bread! I made pumpkin bread dozens of times, and it just wasn't 100 percent. But every baking cookbook needs a delicious pumpkin recipe, so I didn't give up. These tried-and-true pumpkin muffins with a streusel top (or on their own) really taste great.

Yeild: 12 muffins

FOR THE BATTER:

1 cup (245 g) pumpkin puree

2 eggs

1 cup (200 g) granulated sugar

1½ teaspoons (7.5 ml) vanilla extract

½ cup (120 ml) vegetable oil

¼ teaspoon (0.6 g) nutmeg

Pinch allspice

½ teaspoon (3 g) kosher salt (Morton's)

1 teaspoon (2 g) ground cinnamon

1¾ cups (259 g) 1:1 gluten-free flour

2 teaspoons (9.2 g) baking powder

FOR THE TOPPING:

1 cup (148 g) 1:1 gluten-free flour

½ cup (115 g) packed light brown sugar

2 tablespoons (26 g) granulated sugar

½ teaspoon (1 g) ground cinnamon

¼ cup (55 g) vegetable or canola butter, room temperature

FOR THE GLAZE (OPTIONAL):

1 cup (120 g) powdered sugar

1 tablespoon (15 ml) oat or pea-protein milk

To make the batter:

1. Place an oven rack in the center position. Preheat your oven to 375°F (190°C) and line a 12-cup muffin tin with liners.

2. In a mixing bowl, combine the pumpkin, eggs, sugar, vanilla, and vegetable oil. Stir until the mixture is smooth and fully incorporated. Add in the nutmeg, allspice, salt, and cinnamon.

3. Gradually incorporate the flour and baking powder into the mixture, mixing until just incorporated. Be careful not to overmix; we want those muffins to be light and fluffy.

4. Carefully divide the muffin batter into your prepared muffin tin, filling each cup equally.

To make the topping:

1. In a separate mixing bowl, mix flour, brown sugar, both sugars, and cinnamon.

2. Add the butter and work it into the mixture until you have crumbs.

3. Sprinkle generously on top of each muffin.

4. Bake for 15 to 20 minutes, or until a toothpick comes out clean when inserted into the center of a muffin. Cool on a cooling rack.

To make the glaze (optional):

1. Mix ingredients until perfectly smooth.

2. Drizzle over the cooled muffins and enjoy.

Monkey Bread

Monkey bread is gooey, sweet, and full of all the best flavors! It's perfect for breakfast, lunch, dinner, dessert, second dessert—I think you get the picture here. It's seriously so good.

Yield: 6 to 8 servings, one 9 x 13-inch (23 x 33-cm) baking dish

FOR THE DOUGH:

1 cup (230 g) dairy-free, plain, unsweetened yogurt

1 teaspoon (2 g) ground cinnamon

1 teaspoon (6 g) kosher salt (Morton's)

1/3 cup (67 g) granulated sugar, divided

2¼ teaspoons or 1 packet (9 g) dry instant yeast

1 tablespoon (20 g) honey

1/2 cup (120 ml) water, warm (110°F [43°C])

6 tablespoons (85 g) vegetable or canola butter, plus more as needed

1/2 cup (120 ml) oat or pea-protein milk

3½ cups (518 g) 1:1 gluten-free flour or (420 g) gluten-free bread flour

FOR ASSEMBLY:

1½ cups (180 g) chopped walnuts

2 cans (11¼ ounces or 320 g each) dairy-free sweetened condensed milk

NOTE

✳ I prefer using a 9 x 13-inch (23 x 33-cm) baking dish to get a great bake on the whole pan of monkey bread. This creates a single layer of dough. You can use a traditional style Bundt pan, but the dough will stick together more.

To make the dough:

1. In a mixing bowl, using a fitted paddle (not a whisk or dough hook), combine yogurt, cinnamon, and salt. Mix until the mixture is smooth and well combined.

2. In a separate, small mixing bowl, add 2½ tablespoons (28 g) of the sugar, yeast, honey, and warm water. Stir briefly and let it sit for 5 minutes until it starts to get a foamy head—if it does not, it did not activate.

3. To a saucepan, combine the butter, the remaining sugar, and milk. Heat the mixture on medium heat until it begins to bubble on the sides (be careful not to boil). Set aside to cool partially.

4. Add the yeast mixture to the yogurt mixture, and then add the milk mixture to that. Add half of the flour and stir, then add the other half and combine. The dough will be quite sticky—it's supposed to be this way.

To assemble:

1. Grease a 9 x 13-inch (23 x 33-cm) baking dish with butter.

2. Sprinkle the chopped walnuts evenly in the baking dish and pour the sweetened condensed milk over them.

3. Use a 1½- to 2-inch (4- to 5-cm) scoop to place portions of the dough on top of the sweetened condensed milk layer.

4. Cover the dish with a towel and allow the dough to rise in a warm spot until it has tripled in size, which typically takes about 1 to 4 hours (this will depend on humidity, temperature, and elevation).

5. Place an oven rack in the center position. Preheat your oven to 350°F (180°C).

6. Bake the dish for 35 to 45 minutes, or until the top is golden brown.

7. Remove from the oven and let rest for 5 minutes in the dish. Flip the sweet, nutty bread onto a serving platter, and enjoy all its deliciousness.

Orange Sweet Rolls

These sweet rolls are the perfect addition to any brunch affair, offering a burst of citrusy freshness combined with a creamy but light indulgence.

Yield: 9 sweet rolls

FOR THE DOUGH:

¼ cup (24 g) orange zest

1 teaspoon (5 ml) cake batter, vanilla, or cream flavor extract

1 cup (230 g) dairy-free sour cream

⅓ cup (67 g) granulated sugar, divided

2¼ teaspoons or 1 packet (9 g) dry instant yeast

1 tablespoon (20 g) honey

1 cup (235 ml) water, warm (110°F [43°C])

½ cup (112 g) vegetable or canola butter

1 teaspoon (6 g) kosher salt (Morton's)

1 cup (235 ml) oat or pea-protein milk

3½ cups (518 g) 1:1 gluten-free flour or (420 g) gluten-free bread flour, plus more as needed

1 pound (455 g) orange marmalade

1 cup (235 ml) dairy-free heavy cream

To make the dough:

1. Grease a 9 x 13-inch (23 x 33-cm) baking dish generously.

2. Fit the mixer with a paddle (not a whisk or dough hook) and a mixing bowl. Mix orange zest, extract, and sour cream.

3. In a separate bowl, combine 2½ tablespoons (28 g) of the sugar, yeast, honey, and warm water. Let it sit for 5 minutes until frothy.

4. In a saucepan over medium heat, melt butter, then add remaining sugar, salt, and milk. Scald the mixture so there are small bubbles, avoiding boiling. Remove from heat and let it cool partially.

5. Pour yeast mixture into the bowl with the sour cream mix. With the mixer running on low speed, gradually add the milk mixture and incorporate completely.

6. Add flour ½ cup (74 g) at a time, ensuring full integration (you may need to scrape down the sides with a spatula). Mix for an additional 3 minutes to help bind the dough.

7. Transfer the dough to a lightly floured surface. Lightly flour the top of the dough, your hands, and a rolling pin. Gently roll the dough out to approximately 9 x 12 inches (23 x 30 cm).

8. Spread on orange marmalade generously, ensuring an even layer.

9. Roll up the dough tightly, cut into 9 pieces, and place in the buttered baking dish. Cover with plastic wrap and a kitchen towel, place in a warm spot, and allow them to rise to one-and-a-half times their original size, roughly 2 to 3 hours (this time frame will vary based on temperature, humidity, and elevation).

10. Drizzle heavy cream around the rolls for extra goodness.

11. Place an oven rack in the center position. Preheat the oven to 350°F (180°C). Bake the rolls for about 30 minutes until golden brown. Let the rolls cool slightly.

FOR THE FROSTING:

½ cup (112 g) vegetable or canola butter, softened

3 cups (360 g) powdered sugar

1 tablespoon (15 ml) oat or pea-protein milk

1 teaspoon (5 ml) vanilla extract

To make the frosting:

1. Combine all the ingredients until smooth.

2. Generously spread the frosting so it creates a delightful topping as it melts over the warm rolls.

NOTE

※ I normally use 1:1 gluten-free flour. If you use this flour, sometimes the rolls will crack on top during the baking process. It won't change the flavor or texture. If you want a prettier, smoother roll, gluten-free bread flour is the best option.

Orange Cranberry Muffins

Long before the pumpkin spice craze, we had cranberry as a classic fall flavor. And for me, there's not much better than bringing some orange zest to go along with it. I make these muffins as written all the time, but have experimented quite a bit as well. They are great with a handful of chocolate chips or white chocolate chips, and pecans or walnuts are a classic addition.

Yield: 12 muffins

¾ cup (150 g) granulated sugar

1 tablespoon (6 g) orange zest

2 eggs

½ cup (112 g) vegetable or canola butter, melted

¾ cup (175 ml) oat or pea-protein milk

2 teaspoons (10 ml) vanilla extract

2 cups (296 g) 1:1 gluten-free flour

½ teaspoon (3 g) kosher salt (Morton's)

1 tablespoon (13.8 g) baking powder

1 cup (100 g) cranberries (fresh or frozen)

VARIATIONS

✳ **Chocolate chip:** Omit the cranberry and orange zest. Add 1½ cups (263 g) dairy-free chocolate chips.

✳ **Lemon poppyseed:** Omit the cranberries. Swap out the orange zest for lemon zest, and add ¼ cup (60 ml) lemon juice and 2 tablespoons (16 g) poppyseeds.

✳ **Blueberry:** Omit the cranberry and orange zest. Add 1½ cups (220 g) blueberries.

1. Place an oven rack in the center position. Preheat your oven to 400°F (200°C) and give your muffin tin a quick spray with nonstick baking spray, or use muffin tin liners.

2. In a stand mixer fitted with a whisk or paddle attachment and a large mixing bowl, mix the sugar and orange zest gently using your fingers. You will start to smell the citrus goodness. Add the eggs, butter, milk, and vanilla. Mix on high until nicely combined.

3. In a separate bowl, mix together the flour, salt, and baking powder.

4. Slowly add the flour mixture to the egg mixture. Mix everything together until the mixture is halfway mixed (you will still see a lot of flour unmixed).

5. Add the fresh or frozen cranberries to the bowl. Mix them in gently until they're just incorporated by folding them softly with a mixing spoon or spatula. Be careful not to overmix.

6. Distribute the batter evenly into the prepared muffin tin. Each muffin tin should be filled three-quarters of the way.

7. Bake for 18 to 20 minutes. You'll know they're ready when a toothpick inserted into the center of a muffin comes out clean. Cool for a couple minutes in the tin before indulging. If there are any leftovers, store them in an airtight container to keep them fresh.

✳

Baked Fruit Donuts

These donuts are incredibly easy to make. Just pick your favorite fruit and get going—you'll have donuts almost as quick as a run to the donut shop on a busy day. And the best part is, the glaze option complements all of them perfectly. But hey, feel free to get creative and customize the glaze with your favorite flavors once you get the hang of it.

Yield: 10 donuts

FOR THE BATTER:

1 egg

½ cup (115 g) packed light brown sugar

¼ cup (60 g) dairy-free sour cream

½ cup (120 ml) oat or pea-protein milk

1 teaspoon (5 ml) vanilla extract

¼ cup (60 ml) vegetable oil

1¾ cups (259 g) 1:1 gluten-free flour

½ teaspoon (2.3 g) baking soda

2 teaspoons (9.2 g) baking powder

½ teaspoon (1 g) ground cinnamon

½ cup fruit of choice (such as [113 g] mashed banana, [145 g] blueberries, or [170 g] fresh, chopped strawberries)

FOR THE GLAZE:

1¼ cups (150 g) powdered sugar

1 teaspoon (5 ml) vanilla extract

1 to 2 tablespoons (15 to 28 ml) oat or pea-protein milk

To make the batter:

1. Place an oven rack in the center position. Preheat your oven to 350°F (180°C) and spray the donut pan with nonstick baking spray.

2. In a stand mixer fitted with a whisk attachment or a paddle attachment and a large mixing bowl, combine the egg, brown sugar, and sour cream. Mix well until all the ingredients are fully incorporated. Add the milk, vanilla, and vegetable oil to the bowl. Mix on high until the wet ingredients are well combined. Scrape down the sides.

3. In a separate bowl, add all the dry ingredients and mix well. Mix the dry ingredients into the wet just until incorporated. Be careful not to overmix; a few lumps are fine.

4. Next, it's time to add the fruity goodness! Stir in your choice of fruit. Make sure the fruit is evenly distributed.

5. Divide the batter evenly into the prepared donut pans, filling each cavity about two-thirds full.

6. Bake for 10 to 12 minutes or until a toothpick inserted into the center of a donut comes out clean. Let cool for about 5 minutes. Carefully flip the donuts out of the pans onto a cooling rack to cool completely.

To make the glaze:

1. In a bowl, combine the powdered sugar and vanilla. Gradually add 1 tablespoon (15 ml) of the milk to the bowl, mixing until smooth. If needed, add an additional tablespoon (15 ml) of milk to achieve desired glaze consistency.

2. Drizzle the glaze over the top of each donut and dig in.

CHAPTER 7

Savory Breads

Soft Baked Pretzels ✳ 145

Zucchini Bread ✳ 147

Pizza Dough ✳ 148

Cornbread ✳ 151

Sweet Potato Biscuits ✳ 152

Bagels ✳ 155

Cheese and Scallion Scones ✳ 156

Dinner Rolls ✳ 159

Cathead Biscuits ✳ 160

Pepperoni Rolls ✳ 163

Buttery Panini Bread ✳ 164

Buttermilk Biscuits ✳ 167

Focaccia ✳ 168

Soft Baked Pretzels

There's just something about baked soft pretzels that makes them the perfect snack. I just love the chewy, doughy texture and classic salty exterior, whether plain or paired with various dips. This recipe can easily be modified to add a little cheese, jalapeño, or different seasonings. Or, even better for those of us with a sweet tooth, brush with butter and sprinkle with cinnamon and sugar.

Yield: 12 pretzels

FOR THE DOUGH:

1⅓ cups (315 ml) water, warm (110°F [43°C])

3 tablespoons (45 g) packed light brown sugar

2¼ teaspoons or 1 packet (9 g) dry instant yeast

3¾ cups (555 g) 1:1 gluten-free flour

1 teaspoon (4.6 g) baking powder

Vegetable oil for greasing the bowl

FOR BOILING:

2 gallons (7.6 L) water

¼ cup (55.2 g) baking soda

2 tablespoons (26 g) granulated sugar

To make the dough:

1. Attach a paddle to the stand mixer. To the bowl, add water, brown sugar, and yeast. Rest for 5 minutes until it becomes frothy (if it does not, the yeast did not activate). Incorporate the remaining ingredients on low speed for about 5 minutes, until you achieve a smooth, elastic dough.

2. Transfer the dough to a bowl lightly greased with vegetable oil, then cover it with both plastic wrap and a kitchen towel. Rest in a warm space to rise for approximately 1 to 3 hours, or until it has doubled in size (the rise time will vary based on temperature, humidity, and elevation).

3. Divide into 12 equal portions. Roll each piece into a rope about 12 inches (30 cm) long and shape them into smaller-sized pretzels. Be mindful not to make them too large, as this can cause them to break during the boiling step.

4. Place an oven rack in the center position. Preheat your oven to 425°F (220°C) and line 2 baking sheets with parchment paper.

To boil:

1. In a large saucepan, bring water to a boil. Add baking soda and sugar, stirring until fully dissolved. Carefully immerse each pretzel into the boiling water using a slotted spoon, one at a time. Initially, they will sink, but as they cook, they will eventually float. When a pretzel floats, carefully remove it with the slotted spoon and place it on the prepared baking sheet.

✳ continued ✳

✳

FOR TOPPING (OPTIONAL):

1 teaspoon (6 g) kosher salt
(Morton's)

3 tablespoons (42 g) vegetable or
canola butter, melted

To make the topping (optional):

1. This next step is optional but does enhance the flavor. Use the pastry brush to generously coat each pretzel with the melted butter and then sprinkle them with salt.

To bake:

1. Bake for 15 to 20 minutes or until golden brown. After baking, allow the pretzels to cool for a moment, then savor your homemade soft baked pretzels!

NOTES

✳ Exercise caution when handling the pretzels in the boiling water to prevent splashing.

✳ These pretzels are best fresh out of the oven. After a few hours, they will start to harden.

Zucchini Bread

Zucchini bread is one of those classic must-have recipes. There's really nothing quite like it and my recipe is not shy with the zucchini. Just don't skip the pressing step to remove the excess liquid. Especially in peak season, the easiest mistake is forgetting that step, and you'll end up with a watery loaf.

Yield: 1 loaf, 9 x 5-inch (23 x 13-cm) pan

1¼ cups (150 g) grated zucchini

1¾ cups (259 g) gluten-free all-purpose baking flour or 1:1 gluten-free flour

2 teaspoons (9.2 g) baking powder

1 teaspoon (6 g) kosher salt (Morton's)

½ teaspoon (2.3 g) baking soda

½ teaspoon (1 g) ground cardamom

½ teaspoon (1 g) ground cinnamon

½ teaspoon (1 g) nutmeg

½ cup (100 g) granulated sugar

⅓ cup (75 g) packed light brown sugar

½ cup (115 g) dairy-free sour cream

1 tablespoon (15 ml) vanilla extract

½ cup (120 ml) vegetable oil

Zest of 1 medium lemon

2 eggs

1. Press the grated zucchini into paper towels to remove the excess moisture. Set aside.

2. Place an oven rack in the center position. Preheat your oven to 350°F (180°C) and generously spray a 9 x 5-inch (23 x 13-cm) loaf pan with nonstick baking spray, ensuring that it's well coated to prevent sticking.

3. In a stand mixer fitted with a paddle attachment and a large mixing bowl, combine the flour, baking powder, salt, baking soda, cardamom, cinnamon, nutmeg, and sugars. Mix thoroughly.

4. In a separate medium-size mixing bowl, combine the sour cream, vanilla, oil, zucchini, lemon zest, and eggs until well combined.

5. Pour the wet ingredient mixture into the bowl with the dry ingredients. Gently fold and mix until fully incorporated. Be careful not to overmix; the goal is to have a uniform batter.

6. Pour the batter into the prepared loaf pan, ensuring even distribution. Bake for 60 to 75 minutes, until a toothpick inserted into the center of the loaf comes out clean or with a few crumbs.

7. Cool completely in the pan. This helps the flavors settle and the bread to firm up. After it has cooled, slice and enjoy.

Pizza Dough

There's so much to love about pizza, but let's talk about the unsung hero anchoring even the pies with the tastiest toppings—the crust. You want it thin? Done. Thicker? Absolutely. Are you feeling like calzones? This recipe has got your back. It's the versatile crust that can do it all. It's so light and airy, with the perfect amount of chew. Now any night can be pizza night.

Yield: 1 large pizza

FOR THE DOUGH:

¾ cup (175 ml) water, warm (110°F [43°C])

1 teaspoon (4 g) granulated sugar

2¼ teaspoons or 1 packet (9 g) dry instant yeast

2 cups (240 g) gluten-free bread flour

1 teaspoon (6 g) kosher salt (Morton's)

¼ cup (60 ml) sparkling water

2 tablespoons (28 ml) olive oil, plus more as needed

FOR ASSEMBLY:

Olive oil

Toppings of choice

¼ cup (55 g) vegetable or canola oil butter, melted

½ teaspoon (2 g) garlic powder

To make the dough:

1. In a small bowl, combine water, sugar, and yeast. Give it a good stir and let it sit for a moment to activate. You'll know it's ready when the top becomes foamy (if it is not, it did not activate).

2. Fit a stand mixer with a paddle attachment. In the stand mixer's bowl, add the flour and salt; mix together thoroughly.

3. Add the sparkling water, the yeast mixture, and the olive oil into the dry ingredients. Mix on medium speed for 3 minutes until everything comes together into a slightly sticky, elastic dough that holds its shape.

4. Generously brush a glass bowl with olive oil. Place your dough in the bowl and give the top a little olive oil love as well. Cover the bowl with plastic wrap and a towel. Find a draft-free spot and let the dough rest for 3 hours until doubled in size.

To assemble:

1. Place an oven rack in the center position. Preheat oven to 425°F (220°C).

2. Roll the dough out as desired—thin, thick, or your favorite shape. Keep in mind the dough will puff up.

3. If you're making a thicker crust pizza, bake the crust for 10 minutes, remove, top your pizza, and place back in the oven for 10 minutes or until the base is crispy. For a normal or thin pizza, brush the top with olive oil and add whatever toppings you would like. Bake until crust is golden brown.

4. Remove pizza from oven. Brush the dough with melted butter and sprinkle on garlic powder. The pizza is best enjoyed the same day, but it will hold up for 1 day stored in the fridge.

NOTE

✳ There are several ways to bake and shape your pizza. You can bake the pizza dough on parchment paper, a metal pan, a baking stone, baking steel, in a ceramic pizza oven, or a cast-iron skillet. If you're baking on a baking stone, pizza oven, or baking steel, I recommend shaping your pizza using cornmeal. This will help the pizza glide off the peel a lot easier versus flour. With bread flour, you run the risk of the pizza sticking to your peel. If you're using a cast-iron skillet, lightly rub olive oil all over the skillet and then add the pizza dough to get a super crispy crust.

✳

Cornbread

This humble recipe holds a special place in my heart—it's truly one of my all-time favorites. It's also one of those first recipes I adapted and tested many times to master when going dairy- and gluten-free. The uniqueness of this cornbread lies in its texture—it's not fluffy and dry like a typical cornbread, nor is it overly dense like a pudding. To me, it's the ideal blend of flavors and consistency. When I finally achieved the perfect balance between traditional cornbread and creamy corn pudding, it felt like a dream come true.

Yield: 8 servings, one 9 x 13-inch (23 x 33-cm) baking dish

1 cup (235 ml) oat or pea-protein milk

2 eggs

½ cup (120 ml) vegetable oil

1 cup (250 g) creamed corn

1¼ cups (250 g) granulated sugar

1 cup (140 g) fine yellow cornmeal (cannot be coarse)

2 cups (296 g) 1:1 gluten-free flour

1 tablespoon (13.8 g) baking powder

1½ teaspoons (9 g) kosher salt (Morton's)

1. Place an oven rack in the center position. Preheat the oven to 375°F (190°C) and spray a 9 x 13-inch (23 x 33-cm) baking dish with nonstick spray.

2. In a stand mixer with a large mixing bowl and a whisk attachment or paddle, mix milk, eggs, vegetable oil, creamed corn, and sugar on high for 3 minutes.

3. In another mixing bowl, add the fine yellow cornmeal, flour, baking powder, and salt. Mix together.

4. Gently fold the dry ingredients into the wet mix. You don't want to overmix—combine just enough to get along!

5. Pour the batter into the prepared baking dish and let it rest for 5 minutes. Bake to a beautiful golden brown, 25 to 35 minutes. To make sure the cornbread is ready, poke a toothpick in the center and make sure it comes out clean. Cool for 10 minutes before slicing.

Sweet Potato Biscuits

No BBQ feast is complete without a biscuit! These sweet potato biscuits are perfect for any time of the day. Through extensive R&D in my house, we've found they are also perfect for breakfast sandwiches.

Yield: 8 to 10 biscuits

¾ cup (175 ml) oat or pea-protein milk

1 tablespoon (15 ml) white vinegar

1 medium sweet potato

2 cups (296 g) 1:1 gluten-free flour, plus more as needed

1½ tablespoons (20.7 g) baking powder

2 teaspoons (12 g) kosher salt (Morton's)

2 tablespoons (16 g) cornstarch or (18 g) arrowroot powder

1 teaspoon (4 g) BBQ seasoning or (3 g) smoked paprika

1 teaspoon (4.6 g) baking soda

2 tablespoons (26 g) granulated sugar

½ cup + 2 tablespoons (140 g) vegetable or canola butter, cold

1. In a small mixing bowl, whisk together the milk and vinegar. Let sit for about 10 minutes to make buttermilk.

2. Cook sweet potato either in the microwave or by baking until soft. Peel, then blend in a food processor or blender until it becomes smooth. There should be about ¾ cup (185 g) of puree.

3. In a large mixing bowl, thoroughly mix all the dry ingredients. Using a pastry cutter, your hands, or a fork, cut the cold butter into the dry mixture until turned into pea-size crumbs.

4. Create a well in the center of the bowl and add the buttermilk and sweet potato. Gently mix everything until just incorporated.

5. Cover the mixture and refrigerate for 1 hour to allow the butter to firm up again. This step helps to maintain the biscuit's texture during baking.

6. Place an oven rack in the center position. Preheat your oven to 400°F (200°C). Get a 12-inch (30-cm) cast-iron skillet or a baking sheet.

7. Lightly flour work surface, rolling pin, hands, and the dough. Roll out the dough to about 1-inch (2.5-cm) thick. Working quickly is key to prevent the butter from softening.

8. Use a biscuit cutter to create 3- or 4-inch (7.5 or 10-cm) biscuits. Arrange biscuits in the skillet or baking sheet and bake for 25 to 28 minutes until they acquire a light golden-brown color on top. Cool briefly before savoring this awesomeness!

NOTES

⁕ A biscuit cutter is the best option. If a coffee mug or something else with a dull edge is used, the biscuits won't rise the same way as a sharp cut.

⁕ You can brush the top of the biscuits with a little buttermilk before baking, or brush with melted butter when you remove them. If you want to make them a little sweeter, sprinkle a cinnamon/sugar mixture on top.

Bagels

This recipe is for those weekends when nothing but a dozen bagels, baked fresh, will do. You can make them whatever flavor you like best—blueberry, everything bagel, sesame, poppyseed, onion, salt, cinnamon and sugar, or even plain. Enjoy with your favorite spread and then use the leftovers to make delicious sandwiches. My biggest tip is this: like most bagels, these are really best eaten the same day. They will hold up for 1 day, but I recommend using the microwave to heat and soften them. Don't forget about bagel bites! You can shape small balls or experiment with different shapes.

Yield: 12 bagels

FOR THE DOUGH:

1¹⁄₃ cups (315 ml) water, warm (110°F [43°C])

¼ cup (50 g) granulated sugar

2¼ teaspoons or 1 packet (9 g) dry instant yeast

3¾ cups (555 g) 1:1 gluten-free flour

1 teaspoon (4.6 g) baking powder

1¹⁄₂ teaspoons (9 g) kosher salt (Morton's)

3 tablespoons (42 g) vegetable or canola butter, room temperature

FOR BOILING:

2 quarts (1.9 L) water

2 tablespoons (40 g) honey

FOR ASSEMBLY:

1 egg

3 tablespoons (45 ml) water

Your favorite seasonings

To make the dough:

1. Line a cookie sheet with parchment paper.

2. In a stand mixer with a paddle attachment and mixing bowl, combine warm water, sugar, and yeast. Let sit for roughly 5 minutes until nice and foamy—if not, the yeast did not activate.

3. Add the remaining dough ingredients and mix on low for 5 minutes.

4. Remove the dough from the bowl. Lightly flour a work surface and cut the dough into 12 pieces. Shape into a ball. Avoid making them too large to prevent breaking in the water bath. Using your finger or the end of a wooden spoon, create a hole in the center. Place the bagels on the cookie sheet, cover with plastic wrap, top with a towel, and set aside to double in size, 1 to 3 hours.

To boil:

1. On the stove, bring a large pot of water and the honey to a boil over medium/high heat. Use a slotted spoon to gently add the bagels to the water. Remove when they float, about 2 minutes.

2. Place the boiled bagels on the cookie sheet.

To assemble:

1. Place an oven rack in the center position. Preheat the oven to 400°F (200°C).

2. Whisk together egg and water in a small bowl. Brush the top of each bagel with the egg wash.

3. Sprinkle with your favorite seasoning or leave plain.

4. Bake for 20 to 25 minutes until golden brown. Cool completely before slicing and enjoying.

Cheese and Scallion Scones

The first time Joe and I ever went to a brunch party was at my girlfriend, Carol's, house. When we showed up, I was blown away by the spread! Picture this: 10 a.m., sipping cocktails, feasting like it's the last meal you will ever eat. That's when I knew brunch was a lifestyle I'd been missing. These scones are tied to that memory, so I just knew I had to re-create them after going dairy- and gluten-free.

Yield: 8 scones

FOR THE DOUGH:

1 cup (235 ml) oat or pea-protein milk

1 tablespoon (15 ml) white vinegar

3¼ cups (481 g) 1:1 gluten-free flour

2½ tablespoons (34.5 g) baking powder

1 teaspoon (6 g) kosher salt (Morton's)

½ teaspoon (1 g) smoked paprika

¼ teaspoon (1 g) garlic powder

½ teaspoon (1 g) onion powder

½ teaspoon (1 g) black pepper

1 teaspoon (4 g) granulated sugar

¾ cup (165 g) vegetable or canola butter, cold and cubed

½ cup (50 g) chopped scallions

1 cup (115 g) shredded dairy-free Cheddar cheese

2 eggs

FOR ASSEMBLY:

1 egg yolk

2 tablespoons (28 ml) oat or pea-protein milk

To make the dough:

1. In a small mixing bowl, whisk together the milk and vinegar. Let sit for about 10 minutes to make buttermilk.

2. In a large mixing bowl, combine all the dry ingredients and mix well. Add the butter and use a pastry cutter or your fingertips to work it into pea-size crumbles. This gives scones their flakiness.

3. Add the scallions, cheese, eggs, and buttermilk. Gently mix until just combined. Do not overmix, as this can make the scones tough.

4. Wrap tightly in plastic wrap or parchment paper and freeze for 30 minutes.

5. Place an oven rack in the center position. Preheat your oven to 425°F (220°C) and line a standard-size cookie sheet with parchment paper.

6. Remove the dough from the freezer and place on the parchment-lined cookie sheet. Shape the dough into a 7-inch (18-cm) diameter disc with a height of approximately 2 inches (5 cm). Using a lightly floured knife or bench scraper, cut the dough into 8 equal wedges, like slicing a pie. Move the wedges away from each other a bit.

To assemble:

1. In a small mixing bowl, mix egg yolk and milk until well combined. Brush the top of the scones with the egg wash.

2. Bake for around 20 to 25 minutes until the tops are golden brown. The baking time may vary slightly, so keep an eye on them to ensure they don't overcook.

3. Cool for a few minutes before serving.

VARIATION

✳ This is a great base for a savory scone. You can add chopped bacon, diced ham, different types of cheeses, and different seasonings.

✳

Dinner Rolls

These dinner rolls are a delightful addition to any meal, offering a soft, fluffy texture and wonderful flavor. Share them with your loved ones or enjoy them yourself. They are best eaten fresh, and don't skip the brush of melted dairy-free butter on top.

Yield: 9 dinner rolls

2 tablespoons (26 g) granulated sugar

1 cup (235 ml) oat or pea-protein milk, warm (110°F [43°C])

2¼ teaspoons or 1 packet (9 g) dry instant yeast

1¾ cups (210 g) gluten-free bread flour

2 teaspoons (9.2 g) baking powder

1 teaspoon (6 g) kosher salt (Morton's)

1 egg

3 tablespoons (42 g) vegetable or canola butter, melted

3 tablespoons (45 ml) sparkling water

1. Grease a 9-muffin tin with nonstick spray.

2. Add sugar, warm milk, and yeast to a small bowl. Stir briefly and set aside for 5 minutes to activate and foam—if it doesn't, the yeast did not activate.

3. Fit the stand mixer with a paddle attachment and mixing bowl. Mix bread flour, baking powder, and salt. Make a well in the center of the dry mixture. Add in egg, melted butter, yeast mixture, and sparkling water. Mix together for a few minutes until fully combined. Don't worry if the mixture appears lumpy; this is normal.

4. Scoop equal-size portions of the dough into 9 prepared muffin tin cups. Cover the tin with a towel and let the dough rise until it triples in size, about 1 to 2 hours. It should rise slightly above the top of the muffin tin.

5. Place an oven rack in the center position. Preheat your oven to 425°F (220°C).

6. Bake for 18 to 22 minutes until the tops turn a beautiful golden brown. Cool in the tin for 10 minutes. Remove them from the tin and enjoy.

Cathead Biscuits

You may be wondering—what is a cathead biscuit? Traditional throughout the South, they are a drop-style biscuit that is savory and bursting with flavor. They needn't actually be as big as a cat's head to be the perfect bread to serve with dinner!

Yield: 12 biscuits

FOR THE DOUGH:

1⅓ cups (315 ml) oat or pea-protein milk, plus more as needed

1 tablespoon (15 ml) white vinegar, plus more as needed

3 cups (444 g) 1:1 gluten-free flour or (360 g) gluten-free all-purpose baking flour

2½ tablespoons (34.5 g) baking powder

1 teaspoon (4 g) granulated sugar

1½ teaspoons (9 g) kosher salt (Morton's)

½ teaspoon (1.5 g) garlic powder

½ teaspoon (1 g) onion powder

¼ teaspoon (0.5 g) black pepper

2 tablespoons (6 g) chives, fresh or (2 g) dried

1 cup + 2 tablespoons (253 g) vegetable or canola butter

FOR THE TOPPING:

1 egg

2 tablespoons (28 ml) water

3 tablespoons (42 g) vegetable or canola butter, melted

1 tablespoon chopped parsley, (4 g) fresh or (1 g) dried

¼ teaspoon (1 g) garlic powder

1. In a small mixing bowl, whisk together the milk and vinegar. Let sit for about 10 minutes to make buttermilk.

2. Line a cookie sheet with parchment paper.

3. In a large mixing bowl, combine all the dry ingredients and chives, and mix thoroughly. Add the cold butter and use a pastry cutter or your fingers to cut the butter into small, pea-size pieces within the mixture. Do not overmix, as these little clumps of butter ensure the flakiness of the biscuits. Pour the buttermilk into the bowl and mix until just combined. If the dough is too dry, mix up a little more buttermilk and add it. Cover the dough with plastic wrap and refrigerate for 30 minutes.

4. Place an oven rack in the center position. Preheat your oven to 425°F (220°C).

5. Whisk the egg and water together in a small bowl to make an egg wash.

6. Using a spoon or scoop, form 12 biscuits. Place them on the prepared cookie sheet and brush the top of each biscuit with the egg wash to give them a glossy finish.

7. Bake for 25 to 30 minutes until the biscuits turn a slight golden brown.

8. Combine the butter and spices.

9. Brush the tops with the melted butter mixture. Rest for 10 minutes and get ready to dig in.

Pepperoni Rolls

While pepperoni may not top my personal favorites list, my husband adores it! This means whenever I prepare pepperoni rolls, I craft a version with ham, which I love. This recipe is incredibly straightforward. You simply roll the dough once, allow it to rise, and then bake to perfection. Enjoy the filling as written or make it your own.

Yield: 4 to 6 servings

½ cup (120 ml) warm water (110°F [43°C])

1½ tablespoons (30 g) honey

2¼ teaspoons or 1 packet (9 g) dry instant yeast

3½ cups (420 g) gluten-free bread flour, plus more as needed

2 teaspoons (12 g) kosher salt (Morton's)

¼ teaspoon (1 g) garlic powder

1 cup (235 ml) oat or pea-protein milk

¼ cup (55 g) vegetable or canola butter, room temperature

1 egg

2 teaspoons (10 ml) olive oil

2 cups (230 g) shredded dairy-free mozzarella cheese

10 slices of pepperoni (due to size differences in pepperoni, you may need to modify)

2 tablespoons (28 g) vegetable or canola butter, melted

NOTES

✳ This recipe can be modified for your favorite flavors. I love making a pesto cheese version.

✳ The rise time will vary depending on temperature, humidity, and elevation.

1. In a small bowl, combine the warm water, honey, and yeast. Set aside. The yeast will become frothy—if it does not, the yeast did not activate.

2. In a separate large mixing bowl, combine the flour, salt, and garlic powder.

3. In a small saucepan, gently heat the milk and butter over low heat. Warm the milk without bringing it to a boil. Remove from heat and let cool partially.

4. Equip your stand mixer with a fitted paddle attachment and mixing bowl. Add the milk mixture, yeast mixture, and egg. Mix slowly. Do not overmix. Scrape to ensure even blending. Once the dough forms and combines, it's ready.

5. Oil a large glass bowl with olive oil and place the dough inside, then cover with plastic wrap and top with a towel. Let the dough rest and rise until doubled in size, about 2 to 3 hours.

6. Line a cookie sheet with parchment paper.

7. Gently place the dough on a floured work surface and roll it out to approximately 9 x 12 inches (23 x 30 cm) in size. Sprinkle a generous amount of shredded mozzarella evenly over the dough. Arrange the pepperoni slices over the cheese.

8. Roll the dough tightly, ensuring the seam is tucked beneath. Place seam-side down on the cookie sheet and cover it with plastic wrap and a towel, allowing it to double in size, 2 to 3 hours.

9. Place an oven rack in the center position. Preheat your oven to 350°F (180°C).

10. Gently brush the top with the remaining 2 tablespoons (28 ml) of melted butter. Bake for 35 to 45 minutes until golden brown.

11. Rest for 20 minutes before slicing. Feel free to serve it with your favorite marinara.

Buttery Panini Bread

This bread came about somewhat by accident. While gluten- and dairy-free baking is challenging already, adding yeast adds another layer of complexity. I was playing around with recipes and this bread emerged as a winner—though admittedly not what I was originally trying to make. Still, this buttery panini bread has an addictive richness with a soft, pillowy texture—the ideal canvas for your favorite sandwich creations.

Yield: 1 loaf

¾ cup (175 ml) warm water (110°F [43°C])

1½ tablespoons (30 g) honey

2¼ teaspoons or 1 packet (9 g) dry instant yeast

2 cups (240 g) gluten-free bread flour

⅓ cup (38 g) tapioca flour

1½ teaspoons (9 g) kosher salt (Morton's)

¼ cup (55 g) vegetable or canola butter, melted, divided

¼ cup (60 ml) sparkling water

1½ teaspoons (7.5 ml) apple cider vinegar

1. In a small bowl, combine the warm water, honey, and yeast. Rest until foamy on top, roughly 3 to 5 minutes. If it does not get foamy, the yeast didn't activate.

2. In a separate large mixing bowl, blend the dry ingredients. Add 2 tablespoons (28 ml) of the melted butter, sparkling water, vinegar, and the yeast mixture. Stir with a wooden spoon until thoroughly blended and cohesive.

3. Line a cookie sheet with parchment paper, transfer the dough, and lightly dust the top with flour. Cover the dough with plastic wrap and a towel, allowing it to rise until it reaches one-and-a-half times its original size, 1 to 3 hours, depending on temperature, humidity, and elevation.

4. Place an oven rack in the center position. Preheat your oven to 400°F (200°C).

5. Brush the top with the remaining melted butter. Bake for 20 to 25 minutes until golden brown. Cool for 30 minutes on the baking sheet before slicing.

Buttermilk Biscuits

Now, let me tell you: When it comes to buttermilk biscuits, I'm not playing games! I'm talking about that slightly crumbly outer layer, with a flaky, tender inside. Don't even think about serving me a puny, sad biscuit; I want height that touches the sky! This recipe is a shout-out to my friend Ashley, a true North Carolinian who schooled me in the art of crafting a bona fide biscuit. I was so stoked to be able to create this awesomeness gluten- and dairy-free.

Yield: 8 biscuits

1 tablespoon (14 g) vegetable or canola butter, melted

1 cup (235 ml) oat or pea-protein milk

1 tablespoon (15 ml) vinegar

2¼ cups (333 g) 1:1 gluten-free flour, plus more as needed

1¼ teaspoons (7.5 g) kosher salt (Morton's)

1 tablespoon (13 g) granulated sugar

½ teaspoon (2.6 g) baking soda

1 tablespoon (13.8 g) baking powder

½ cup (112 g) vegetable or canola butter, cold and cubed

1. Place an oven rack in the center position. Preheat your oven to 450°F (230°C) and brush a cast-iron skillet or 7 x 10-inch (18 x 25-cm) baking dish with melted butter.

2. In a small mixing bowl, whisk together the milk and vinegar. Let sit for about 10 minutes to make buttermilk. Reserve 1 tablespoon (15 ml) for brushing the biscuit tops later.

3. In a large mixing bowl, assemble all your dry ingredients. Mix completely. Cut the cold butter in with your hands or a pastry cutter. Do not overmix; leave pea-size butter pieces in the dough.

4. Make a well and add buttermilk. Gently stir until everything just comes together. Be cautious not to overmix; it's all about maintaining that biscuit finesse. Wrap your biscuit dough tightly with plastic wrap and refrigerate for 1 hour or freeze for 20 minutes.

5. Lightly flour the work surface, your dough, rolling pin, biscuit cutter, and hands. Roll out the chilled dough until it's about 1-inch (2.5 cm) thick. Using a 3- or 4-inch (7.5 or 10-cm) biscuit cutter (trust me, this makes all the difference), cut out 8 biscuits. Avoid using a cup or similar objects; it's the biscuit cutter that gives you those fabulous flaky edges.

6. Place the cut biscuits in your prepared skillet or baking dish and brush them with the reserved buttermilk. This helps the biscuits to achieve their golden crust.

7. Bake for 17 to 22 minutes until the tops are a light golden brown. Cool in the skillet or dish for 10 minutes before removing.

Focaccia

Any type of bread that includes yeast can be tricky to master. My goal for all the bread recipes in this cookbook was to make baking them as easy and pleasurable as possible. Thus, this focaccia is meant to be one that can turn out perfect even on the first bake! It has a crispy exterior and a soft, bouncy interior. Soon, you'll be wanting to use this bread to make all your sandwiches!

Yield: 8 to 10 servings, one 9 x 13-inch (23 x 33-cm) baking dish

FOR THE DOUGH:

1 cup (235 ml) water, warm (around 110°F [43°C])

2 teaspoons (13 g) honey

2¼ teaspoons or 1 packet (9 g) dry instant yeast

3¾ cups (450 g) gluten-free bread flour

1 teaspoon (4.6 g) baking powder

2 teaspoons (12 g) kosher salt (Morton's)

2 teaspoons (2 g) herbes de Provence

5 tablespoons (75 ml) olive oil, divided

1 cup (235 ml) sparkling water

FOR ASSEMBLY:

2 tablespoons (28 ml) olive oil

½ cup (50 g) dairy-free Parmesan cheese

1 teaspoon (1 g) herbes de Provence

1½ teaspoons (6 g) fleur de sel

To make the focaccia:

1. Mix together warm water, honey, and yeast in a small bowl. Set aside for 5 minutes until the top is very foamy—if it isn't, it did not activate.

2. In a large mixing bowl, combine dry ingredients. Make a well in the center and pour in 3 tablespoons (45 ml) of the olive oil, sparkling water, and the yeast mixture. Mix until fully incorporated. If the dough seems sticky and lumpy, that's fine.

3. Generously coat a 9 x 13-inch (23 x 33-cm) baking dish with 2-inch (5-cm) sides using 2 more tablespoons (28 ml) of the olive oil. A metal pan will yield the crispiest sides. Line it with parchment paper, allowing it to extend up the long sides; this makes it easier to lift out your focaccia later.

4. Place dough in the baking dish. Use olive oil on your fingers and spread out the dough. Spray one side of a piece of plastic wrap with nonstick spray and lay it on top of the dough, followed by a towel. Allow dough to rise in a warm spot until it triples in size, 1 to 3 hours (depending on temperature, humidity, and elevation).

To assemble:

1. Place an oven rack in the center position. Preheat your oven to a toasty 425°F (220°C).

2. Drizzle olive oil over the entire top. Distribute toppings evenly to create layers of flavor.

3. Bake for 25 to 30 minutes until the top turns golden brown. Cool for 20 minutes in the dish before removing. You may need to use a knife to separate the bread from the dish. Cool for 30 minutes before slicing.

✳ **continued** ✳

NOTES

⁎ Focaccia can be made in different shapes. You could also use two 9-inch (9-cm) round pans. Regardless, don't overcrowd the pan, or your focaccia won't have room to rise. The sides of any baking dish used should be at least 2 inches (5 cm) high.

⁎ The key to an incredible focaccia is great ingredients. I recommend splurging on really good-quality olive oil and toppings. Good olives, seasonings, and cheeses will take this up a major notch. This bread can be customized to what's in your pantry/fridge once you get the hang of it. Swap out the seasoning for your favorites, or add a different cheese.

Resources

✳ Bob's Red Mill is my ultimate go-to for gluten-free flour. Their gluten-free 1.1 flour and all-purpose flour are my go-to choice for all my cooking and baking needs. They're trustworthy and always delivers excellent results!
Shop here: https://www.bobsredmill.com/

✳ Spread the Love crafts exceptional nut butters that I can't get enough of! You guys know I'm a peanut butter addict, they are hands down my favorite choice! Their products are staples in my baking recipes, precisely delivering the flavors and quality I seek in every creation.
Shop here: https://www.spreadthelovefoods.com/

✳ Grandy Organics has amazing pantry staples including their oats. I always keep their oats (and granolas) in my pantry.
Shop here: https://www.grandyorganics.com/

✳ Nellie's Eggs are my recipe essentials! The convenience of finding them at nearly every grocery store is a game-changer, and their quality always enhances the taste of my dishes.
Store locator here: https://www.nelliesfreerange.com/

✳ Amoretti's extensive product line is impressive, catering to nearly all my needs for creativity. When it comes to extracts, syrups, or unique flours, they are just right. They are high quality and one of my absolute favorite pantry staples.
Shop here: https://www.amoretti.com/

✳ Kite Hill offers top-notch dairy-free cream cheese, sour cream, and ricotta that works perfectly for my baking and no-bake recipes. Their consistency and quality provide what I need for my culinary creations.
Store locator here: https://www.kite-hill.com/

✳ Fat Daddio's offers an extensive range of baking sheets, cooking pans, and oven-related essentials. Their collections stand out, and I genuinely appreciate the quality and variety of their products.
Shop here: https://www.fatdaddios.com/

✳ Nordic Ware, renowned for its diverse bundt pan collection, now offers an array of high-quality baking pans. While Bundt options remain a highlight, their selection includes top-notch standard and specialty pans, meeting various baking needs.
Shop here: https://www.nordicware.com/

✳

Acknowledgments

I am dedicating this cookbook to my girlfriend, Brittany. She encouraged me to start an Instagram page and start sharing my recipes.

I also want to express my deep appreciation to my husband for his support throughout this creative process. Thank you, Joe.

Additionally, I extend my appreciation to my dedicated team, Carol and Amanda. Their dedication, collaboration, and unwavering commitment made this cookbook process much easier. This cookbook is proof of the power of teamwork—without everyone, this wouldn't have been possible.

About the Author

DANIELLE COCHRAN is a professional recipe developer, food photographer, and content creator. Her brand, The Salty Cooker, focuses on high-quality gluten- and dairy-free recipes that everyone will enoy. From breakfast to 20-minute meals, grilling, smoking, and elegant bakes—and, of course, spectacular desserts—she continually strives to make her creations irresistible for everyone. Her approachable style and rigorous recipe testing makes it easy for her readers to re-create the recipes at home. Her passion for sharing recipes using the best ingredients has also led to coverage by *Taste of Home*, The Feedfeed, *Taste of the South*, and *Southern Cast Iron*, as well as work with multiple brand partners, including Tastemade, D'Artagnan, and Canyon Bakehouse. Find her online as @thesaltycooker or at https://www.thesaltycooker.com/.

When she isn't working, she loves spending time with her husband Joe, their two dogs, and their friends. Danielle enjoys fishing, traveling, kayaking, going out to eat, and new adventures! As much as Danielle loves to travel she is also a homebody.

Index

A

almond flour: Cherry Hazelnut Biscotti, 24
almonds: Pear Frangipane, 114
apples
    Apple Sticky Buns, 125–127
    Classic Apple Oatmeal Cookies, 27
    Dutch Apple Pie, 113
applesauce: Apple Sticky Buns, 125–127

B

bananas
    Baked Fruit Donuts, 140
    Banana Bread Cinnamon Rolls with
        Peanut Butter Frosting, 119–120
    Banana Bread Cookies, 30
    Bananas Foster Cheesecake, 83
    Hummingbird Cake, 49
    measurement conversions, 11
blackberries
    Champagne Swiss Roll with Swiss
        Meringue Frosting, 63–65
    French Fruit Tart, 110–111
blueberries
    Baked Fruit Donuts, 140
    Blueberry Muffins, 139
    Champagne Swiss Roll with Swiss
        Meringue Frosting, 63–65
    French Fruit Tart, 110–111
    Lemon Bundt Cake with Blueberry
        Swirl, 60–61
    Tangy Lemon Cheesecake with
        Blueberry Sauce, 91
butter
    substitutions for, 16
    tips and tricks, 17
buttermilk
    Buttermilk Biscuits, 167
    Cathead Biscuits, 160–61
    Cheese and Scallion Scones, 156–157
    Peach Cobbler, 100
    substitutions for, 13
    Sweet Potato Biscuits, 152

C

caramel
    Chocolate Caramel Revel Bars, 23
    Flan, 88
    Turtle Chocolate Chip Skillet Cookie, 41
champagne: Champagne Swiss Roll with
    Swiss Meringue Frosting, 63–65
Cheddar cheese: Cheese and Scallion
    Scones, 156–157
cherries
    Black Forest Mini Cheesecake Bites, 87
    Cherry Hazelnut Biscotti, 24
    Upside-Down Pineapple Cake, 50

chocolate
    Black Forest Mini Cheesecake Bites, 87
    Bread Pudding with Chocolate
        Chips, 128
    Chocolate Cake Every Which
        Way, 69–71
    Chocolate Caramel Revel Bars, 23
    Chocolate Chip Muffins, 139
    Chocolate Chip Walnut Cookies, 33
    Chocolate Coconut Tres Leches
        Cake, 53
    Éclairs, 104–105
    Gooey S'mores Brownies, 38
    Peanut Butter Cookie Sandwiches, 42
    Strawberry Shortcake Blondie Bars, 37
    substitutions for, 14
    Turtle Chocolate Chip Skillet Cookie, 41
cocoa powder
    Chocolate Cake Every Which
        Way, 69–71
    Chocolate Coconut Tres Leches
        Cake, 53
    Gooey S'mores Brownies, 38
    Red Velvet Cupcakes with Cream
        Cheese Frosting, 66
    substitutions for, 14
coconut
    Basque Cheesecake with Strawberry
        Sauce, 84
    Chocolate Coconut Tres Leches Cake, 53
    Coconut Cake with Raspberry
        Filling, 56–57
    German Chocolate Frosting, 71
    Hummingbird Cake, 49
coffee
    Chocolate Cake Every Which
        Way, 69–71
    Red Velvet Cupcakes with Cream
        Cheese Frosting, 66
corn: Cornbread, 151
cranberries: Orange Cranberry Muffins, 139
cream cheese
    Banana Bread Cinnamon Rolls with
        Peanut Butter Frosting, 119–120
    Banana Bread Cookies, 30
    Bananas Foster Cheesecake, 83
    Basque Cheesecake with Strawberry
        Sauce, 84
    Black Forest Mini Cheesecake Bites, 87
    Classic Cinnamon Rolls, 121
    Coconut Cake with Raspberry
        Filling, 56–57
    Gingerbread Cupcakes with Cinnamon
        Cream Cheese Frosting, 58–59
    Hummingbird Cake, 49
    Peaches and Cream Cheesecake Bars, 80
    Peanut Butter Frosting, 71

    Pecan Pie Cheesecake Bars, 92
    Rainbow Confetti Cheesecake, 79
    Red Velvet Cupcakes with Cream
        Cheese Frosting, 66
    Sour Cream Coffee Cake, 123–124
    Tangy Lemon Cheesecake with
        Blueberry Sauce, 91
    temperature of, 19
    Vanilla Bean Cheesecake, 95

D

dairy-free substitutions, 15–16
dates
    Sticky Date Pudding, 76
    substitutions for, 14

E

eggs
    Angel Food Cake, 68
    Bagels, 155
    Baked Fruit Donuts, 140
    Banana Bread Cookies, 30
    Bananas Foster Cheesecake, 83
    Basque Cheesecake with Strawberry
        Sauce, 84
    Black Forest Mini Cheesecake Bites, 87
    Bread Pudding with Chocolate
        Chips, 128
    Cathead Biscuits, 160–61
    Champagne Swiss Roll with Swiss
        Meringue Frosting, 63–65
    Cheese and Scallion Scones, 156–157
    Cherry Hazelnut Biscotti, 24
    Chocolate Cake Every Which
        Way, 69–71
    Chocolate Caramel Revel Bars, 23
    Chocolate Chip Walnut Cookies, 33
    Chocolate Coconut Tres Leches
        Cake, 53
    Citrus Olive Oil Cake, 62
    Classic Apple Oatmeal Cookies, 27
    Coconut Cake with Raspberry
        Filling, 56–57
    cookies and bars, 28
    Cornbread, 151
    Cream Puffs with Butterscotch Pastry
        Cream, 103
    Dinner Rolls, 159
    Éclairs, 104–105
    Flan, 88
    French Fruit Tart, 110–111
    French Vanilla Scones, 131
    German Chocolate Frosting, 71
    Gingerbread Cupcakes with Cinnamon
        Cream Cheese Frosting, 58–59
    Gooey S'mores Brownies, 38
    Hummingbird Cake, 49

*

eggs, continued
    Key Lime Pie, 109
    Lemon Bars, 45
    Lemon Bundt Cake with Blueberry
        Swirl, 60–61
    Orange Cranberry Muffins, 139
    Orange Creamsicle Cupcakes, 54
    Peaches and Cream Cheesecake Bars, 80
    Peanut Butter Cookie Sandwiches, 42
    Pear Frangipane, 114
    Pecan Pie Cheesecake Bars, 92
    Pepperoni Rolls, 163–65
    Pumpkin Streusel Muffins, 132
    Rainbow Confetti Cheesecake, 79
    Raspberry Pistachio Galette, 106
    Red Velvet Cupcakes with Cream
        Cheese Frosting, 66
    Snickerdoodle Cookies, 28
    Sour Cream Coffee Cake, 123–124
    Sticky Date Pudding, 76
    Strawberry Rhubarb Pie, 98–99
    Strawberry Shortcake Blondie Bars, 37
    substitutions for, 14
    Tangy Lemon Cheesecake with
        Blueberry Sauce, 91
    temperature of, 17
    Turtle Chocolate Chip Skillet Cookie, 41
    Upside-Down Pineapple Cake, 50
    Vanilla Bean Cheesecake, 95
    Vanilla Crème Brûlée, 75
    whipping tips, 19
    Zucchini Bread, 147
evaporated milk
    Chocolate Coconut Tres Leches Cake, 53
    German Chocolate Frosting, 71

F
frosting
    Banana Bread Cinnamon Rolls with
        Peanut Butter Frosting, 119–120
    Banana Bread Cookies, 30
    Champagne Swiss Roll with Swiss
        Meringue Frosting, 63–65
    Chocolate Cake Every Which
        Way, 69–71
    Classic Cinnamon Rolls, 121
    Coconut Cake with Raspberry Filling, 56
    German Chocolate Frosting, 71
    Gingerbread Cupcakes with Cinnamon
        Cream Cheese Frosting, 58–59
    Hummingbird Cake, 49
    Orange Creamsicle Cupcakes, 54
    Orange Sweet Rolls, 136–137
    Peanut Butter Frosting, 71
    Rainbow Confetti Cheesecake, 79
    Red Velvet Cupcakes with Cream
        Cheese Frosting, 66
    substitutions for, 14
    tips and tricks, 19

G
ginger: Gingerbread Cupcakes with
    Cinnamon Cream Cheese
    Frosting, 58–59
gluten-free substitutions, 16
graham crackers
    Bananas Foster Cheesecake, 83
    Gooey S'mores Brownies, 38
    Key Lime Pie, 109
    Pecan Pie Cheesecake Bars, 92
    Tangy Lemon Cheesecake with
        Blueberry Sauce, 91
    Vanilla Bean Cheesecake, 95
Grand Marnier: Basque Cheesecake with
    Strawberry Sauce, 84

H
hazelnuts
    Cherry Hazelnut Biscotti, 24
    Peanut Butter Cookie Sandwiches, 42
heavy cream
    Banana Bread Cinnamon Rolls with
        Peanut Butter Frosting, 119–120
    Bread Pudding with Chocolate
        Chips, 128
    Classic Cinnamon Rolls, 121
    Cream Puffs with Butterscotch Pastry
        Cream, 103
    Gingerbread Cupcakes with Cinnamon
        Cream Cheese Frosting, 58–59
    Orange Sweet Rolls, 136–137
    Pecan Pie Cheesecake Bars, 92
    Sticky Date Pudding, 76
    substitution for, 13
    Vanilla Crème Brûlée, 75
honey
    Apple Sticky Buns, 125–127
    Bagels, 155
    Banana Bread Cinnamon Rolls with
        Peanut Butter Frosting, 119–120
    Buttery Panini Bread, 164
    Classic Cinnamon Rolls, 121
    Focaccia, 168–170
    Monkey Bread, 135
    Orange Sweet Rolls, 136–137
    Pepperoni Rolls, 163–65

K
kiwi: French Fruit Tart, 110–111

L
lemons
    Basque Cheesecake with Strawberry
        Sauce, 84
    Citrus Olive Oil Cake, 62
    Dutch Apple Pie, 113
    Lemon Bars, 45
    Lemon Bundt Cake with Blueberry
        Swirl, 60–61
    Lemon Poppyseed Muffins, 139
    substitution for, 13

    Tangy Lemon Cheesecake with
        Blueberry Sauce, 91
    Zucchini Bread, 147
limes
    Citrus Olive Oil Cake, 62
    Key Lime Pie, 109

M
macadamia nuts: Key Lime Pie, 109
marshmallow fluff: Gooey S'mores
    Brownies, 38
measurements, 10–11
milk, substitutions for, 13, 15
molasses: Gingerbread Cupcakes with
    Cinnamon Cream Cheese
    Frosting, 58–59
mozzarella cheese: Pepperoni Rolls, 163–65

O
oat milk
    Apple Sticky Buns, 125–127
    Baked Fruit Donuts, 140
    Banana Bread Cinnamon Rolls with
        Peanut Butter Frosting, 119–120
    Bread Pudding with Chocolate Chips, 128
    Buttermilk Biscuits, 167
    Cathead Biscuits, 160–61
    Cheese and Scallion Scones, 156–157
    Chocolate Cake Every Which
        Way, 69–71
    Chocolate Coconut Tres Leches Cake, 53
    Classic Cinnamon Rolls, 121
    Coconut Cake with Raspberry
        Filling, 56–57
    Cornbread, 151
    Dinner Rolls, 159
    Éclairs, 104–105
    Flan, 88
    French Fruit Tart, 110–111
    Gingerbread Cupcakes with Cinnamon
        Cream Cheese Frosting, 58–59
    Monkey Bread, 135
    Orange Cranberry Muffins, 139
    Orange Creamsicle Cupcakes, 54
    Orange Sweet Rolls, 136–137
    Pepperoni Rolls, 163–65
    Pumpkin Streusel Muffins, 132
    Red Velvet Cupcakes with Cream
        Cheese Frosting, 66
    Sweet Potato Biscuits, 152
oats
    Chocolate Caramel Revel Bars, 23
    Classic Apple Oatmeal Cookies, 27
    Dutch Apple Pie, 113
    Peanut Butter and Jelly Oatmeal Bars, 34
oranges
    Basque Cheesecake with Strawberry
        Sauce, 84
    Citrus Olive Oil Cake, 62
    Coconut Cake with Raspberry Filling,
        56–57

Gingerbread Cupcakes with Cinnamon Cream Cheese Frosting, 58–59
Orange Cranberry Muffins, 139
Orange Creamsicle Cupcakes, 54
Orange Sweet Rolls, 136–137
Strawberry Rhubarb Pie, 98–99

P

Parmesan cheese: Focaccia, 168–170
peaches
    Peach Cobbler, 100
    Peaches and Cream Cheesecake Bars, 80
peanut butter
    Banana Bread Cinnamon Rolls with Peanut Butter Frosting, 119–120
    Peanut Butter and Jelly Oatmeal Bars, 34
    Peanut Butter Cookie Sandwiches, 42
    Peanut Butter Frosting, 71
    substitutions for, 14
pea-protein milk
    Apple Sticky Buns, 125–127
    Baked Fruit Donuts, 140
    Banana Bread Cinnamon Rolls with Peanut Butter Frosting, 119–120
    Bread Pudding with Chocolate Chips, 128
    Buttermilk Biscuits, 167
    Cathead Biscuits, 160–61
    Cheese and Scallion Scones, 156–157
    Chocolate Cake Every Which Way, 69–71
    Chocolate Coconut Tres Leches Cake, 53
    Classic Cinnamon Rolls, 121
    Coconut Cake with Raspberry Filling, 56–57
    Cornbread, 151
    Dinner Rolls, 159
    Éclairs, 104–105
    Flan, 88
    French Fruit Tart, 110–111
    Gingerbread Cupcakes with Cinnamon Cream Cheese Frosting, 58–59
    Monkey Bread, 135
    Orange Cranberry Muffins, 139
    Orange Creamsicle Cupcakes, 54
    Orange Sweet Rolls, 136–137
    Pepperoni Rolls, 163–65
    Pumpkin Streusel Muffins, 132
    Red Velvet Cupcakes with Cream Cheese Frosting, 66
    Sweet Potato Biscuits, 152
pears: Pear Frangipane, 114
pecans
    Apple Sticky Buns, 125–127
    Dutch Apple Pie, 113
    German Chocolate Frosting, 71
    Hummingbird Cake, 49
    Pecan Pie Cheesecake Bars, 92
    Sour Cream Coffee Cake, 123–124
    substitutions for, 14
    Turtle Chocolate Chip Skillet Cookie, 41
pepperoni: Pepperoni Rolls, 163–65
pineapple
    Hummingbird Cake, 49
    Upside-Down Pineapple Cake, 50

pistachios: Raspberry Pistachio Galette, 106
pretzels: Soft Baked Pretzels, 145–146
pumpkin: Pumpkin Streusel Muffins, 132
pumpkin pie spice: substitutions for, 14

R

raspberries
    Champagne Swiss Roll with Swiss Meringue Frosting, 63–65
    Coconut Cake with Raspberry Filling, 56–57
    French Fruit Tart, 110–111
    Raspberry Pistachio Galette, 106
rhubarb: Strawberry Rhubarb Pie, 98–99
rum
    Bananas Foster Cheesecake, 83
    as vanilla substitute, 13

S

scallions: Cheese and Scallion Scones, 156–157
sour cream
    Baked Fruit Donuts, 140
    Bananas Foster Cheesecake, 83
    Chocolate Cake Every Which Way, 69–71
    Citrus Olive Oil Cake, 62
    Classic Cinnamon Rolls, 121
    Dutch Apple Pie, 113
    Lemon Bundt Cake with Blueberry Swirl, 60–61
    Orange Creamsicle Cupcakes, 54
    Orange Sweet Rolls, 136–137
    Pecan Pie Cheesecake Bars, 92
    Rainbow Confetti Cheesecake, 79
    Raspberry Pistachio Galette, 106
    Sour Cream Coffee Cake, 123–124
    Strawberry Rhubarb Pie, 98–99
    substitution for, 13
    Tangy Lemon Cheesecake with Blueberry Sauce, 91
    Upside-Down Pineapple Cake, 50
    Vanilla Bean Cheesecake, 95
    Zucchini Bread, 147
sprinkles: Rainbow Confetti Cheesecake, 79
strawberries
    Baked Fruit Donuts, 140
    Basque Cheesecake with Strawberry Sauce, 84
    Champagne Swiss Roll with Swiss Meringue Frosting, 63–65
    Chocolate Coconut Tres Leches Cake, 53
    French Fruit Tart, 110–111
    Peanut Butter and Jelly Oatmeal Bars, 34
    Strawberry Rhubarb Pie, 98–99
    Strawberry Shortcake Blondie Bars, 37
substitutions, 13–14, 15–16
sweetened condensed milk
    Chocolate Caramel Revel Bars, 23
    Chocolate Coconut Tres Leches Cake, 53
    Monkey Bread, 135
    Turtle Chocolate Chip Skillet Cookie, 41

sweet potatoes: Sweet Potato Biscuits, 152

T

temperatures, 11
tips and tricks, 17–19
tools and equipment, 12–13

V

vanilla cream: Orange Creamsicle Cupcakes, 54

W

walnuts
    Banana Bread Cookies, 30
    Bananas Foster Cheesecake, 83
    Chocolate Chip Walnut Cookies, 33
    Monkey Bread, 135
    substitutions for, 14
weight measurements, 11
whipped topping
    Chocolate Coconut Tres Leches Cake, 53
    Key Lime Pie, 109
    Peaches and Cream Cheesecake Bars, 80
    Rainbow Confetti Cheesecake, 79
white chocolate: Strawberry Shortcake Blondie Bars, 37

Y

yeast
    Apple Sticky Buns, 125–127
    Bagels, 155
    Banana Bread Cinnamon Rolls with Peanut Butter Frosting, 119–120
    Buttery Panini Bread, 164
    Dinner Rolls, 159
    Focaccia, 168–170
    Monkey Bread, 135
    Orange Sweet Rolls, 136–137
    Pepperoni Rolls, 163–65
    Pizza Dough, 148–149
    Soft Baked Pretzels, 145–146
    tips and tricks, 18
yogurt
    Apple Sticky Buns, 125–127
    Classic Cinnamon Rolls, 121
    Coconut Cake with Raspberry Filling, 56–57
    Monkey Bread, 135
    substitutions for, 13

Z

zucchini: Zucchini Bread, 147